ROME

North American edition first published in 2008 by:

The Rosen Publishing Group, Inc.
29 E. 21st Street
New York, NY 10010

North American edition copyright © 2008 by The Rosen Publishing Group, Inc. First published as *Rome: The Greatest Empire of the Ancient World* in the United Kingdom, copyright © 2005 by Carlton Books Limited. Text copyright © 2005 by Nick McCarty. Additional end matter copyright © 2008 by The Rosen Publishing Group, Inc.

Design: Mercer Design
Senior Designer: Vicky Holmes
Project Editor: Amie McKee
Picture Research: Steve Behan
Production: Lisa Moore

Library of Congress Cataloging-in-Publication Data

McCarty, Nick, 1940–
Rome / Nick McCarty.
    p. cm.—(Prime time history)
ISBN-13: 978-1-4042-1366-1 (library binding)
1. Rome—History—Juvenile literature. 2. Rome—History, Military—Juvenile literature. 3. Rome—Social life and customs—Juvenile literature. I. Title. II. Series.
DG209.M39 2008
937—dc22

                                                                            2007033501

Manufactured in the United States of America

PRIME TIME HISTORY™

ROME

THE GREATEST EMPIRE OF THE ANCIENT WORLD

NICK McCARTY

ROSEN
PUBLISHING®
New York

Picture Credits

The publishers would like to thank the following sources for their kind permission to reproduce the pictures in the book.

(T = Top, B = Bottom and M = Middle)

Endpaper: Corbis / Bettmann; **1:** Getty Images / *Three Lions*; **3:** Bridgeman Art Library / Sarcophagus of Cornelius Statius depicting scenes from the life of a child (marble), Roman (2nd century CE) / Louvre, Paris, France; **10:** Bridgeman Art Library / *The Reconstruction of Ancient Rome at the Time of the Antonines*, c. 1819 (pen & ink and w/c on paper), Cockerell, Charles Robert (1788–1863) / Private Collection, Credit: Charles Plante Fine Arts; **11:** Alinari Picture Library; **12:** Topfoto.co.uk; **13:** Sonia Halliday Photographs; **14:** © The Bridgeman Art Library/Getty Images; **16:** AKG Images / Erich Lessing; **18:** AKG Images; **19:** Bridgeman Art Library / Map of Rome, from *Civitates Orbis Terrarum* by Georg Braun (1541–1622) and Frans Hogenberg (1535–1590), c. 1572 (colored engraving), Hoefnagel, Joris (1542–1600) (after) / Private Collection, Credit: The Stapleton Collection; **20:** Corbis / Gianni Dagli Orti; **21t:** AKG Images; **21m:** The Art Archive / Dagli Orti; **22:** AKG Images / Peter Connolly; **23:** Alinari Picture Library; **24:** Bridgeman Art Library / *The Taking of Thelesia by Hannibal and His Army*, 1860 (oil on canvas), Masson, Benedict (1819–93) / Private Collection, Credit: Archives Charmet; **25:** Getty Images / Mansell / Time Life Pictures; **26:** AKG Images / Erich Lessing; **27:** AKG Images; **28:** Getty Images / *Three Lions*; **30:** © Imagno/Hulton Archive/Getty Images; **31:** AKG Images / Rabatti-Domingie; **32:** Getty Images / Hulton Archive; **33t:** Bridgeman Art Library / *Reception in the Senate*, detail from the Arch of Trajan (marble), Benevento, Campania, Italy, Credit: INDEX; **33b:** AKG Images; **34:** Topfoto.co.uk; **36:** AKG Images / Erich Lessing; **38:** Corbis / Archivo Icongrafico, S.A.; **39:** AKG Images; **41:** AKG Images; **42:** AKG Images / Rabatti-Domingie; **43:** Alinari Picture Library; **44:** Alinari Picture Library; **45:** AKG Images / Erich Lessing; **46:** Corbis / Patrick Ward; **47:** Getty Images / Hulton Archive; **48/49:** Corbis / Bettmann; **50:** Bridgeman Art Library / *Alesia Besieged by Julius Caesar* (101–44 BCE) (oil on panel), Feselen, Melchior (d. 1538) / Alte Pinakothek, Munich, Germany, Lauros / Giraudon; **51:** Bridgeman Art Library /Model of Caesar's defenses at Alesia (mixed media), French School, (19th century) / Musee des Antiquites Nationales, St-Germain-en-Laye, France, Lauros / Giraudon; **52:** Bridgeman Art Library /Helmet with cheek guards, from Alesia, Tene III (bronze), Gaulish (1st century BCE) / Musee des Antiquites Nationales, St-Germain-en-Laye, France, Lauros / Giraudon; **53t:** Corbis / Bettmann; **53b:** Topfoto.co.uk; **54:** Bridgeman Art Library / Frontispiece to *Pharsalia* or *The Civil War Between Caesar and Pompey* by Marcus Annaeus Lucan (39–65 CE) engraved by J. Cole, 1719 (engraving), English School (18th century), Private Collection; **56:** AKG Images; **57:** Topfoto.co.uk / The British Museum / HIP; **58:** Bridgeman Art Library /Julius Caesar (100–44 BCE) Crossing the Rubicon c. 1470 (vellum) (detail), Fouquet, Jean (c. 1420–80) / Louvre, Paris, France, Giraudon; **59:** Bridgeman Art Library /Cassone, with painted side panel depicting the Battle of Pharsalia from the *History of Pompey and Caesar*, Florentine School, 15th century (wood, gilded and painted in tempera) (see also 71848), Samuel Courtauld Trust, Courtauld Institute of Art Gallery; **60:** Bridgeman Art Library /Relief depicting a funeral scene (stone), Roman (1st century CE) / Museo della Civilta Romana, Rome, Italy, Giraudon; **61t:** Corbis / Sandro Vannini; **61b:** Bridgeman Art Library / *Triumph of Caesar* Fresco - detail I (b/w engraving of fresco), Mantegna, Andrea (1431–1506) / British Library, London, UK; **62:** Corbis / Bettmann; **64:** Alinari Picture Library; **65:** AKG Images / Pirozzi; **66:** Corbis / Arte & Immagini srl; **67:** Bridgeman Art Library / Julius Caesar (100–44 BCE) on his way to the Senate on the Ides of March (oil on canvas) (study), Pujol, Abel de (1787–1861) / Musee des Beaux-Arts, Valenciennes, France, Lauros / Giraudon; **68/69:** Bridgeman Art Library / *The Death of Caesar* (100–44 BCE) (oil on paper), Lethiere, Guillaume (1760–1832) / Private Collection; **70:** Bridgeman Art Library / The Battle of Actium, 2nd September 31 BC, 1600 (mural), Vassilacchi, Antonio (1556–1629) / Villa Barbarigo, Noventa Vicentina, Italy, Giraudon; **72:** Bridgeman

Art Library / *The Young Octavian* Bust of the Emperor Augustus (63 BCE–14 CE), c. 1800 (marble), Canova, Antonio (1757–1822) (after) / Private Collection, Credit: Philip Mould, Historical Portraits Ltd, London, UK; **74t:** Bridgeman Art Library / *The Death of Brutus*, 1793 (oil on canvas), Guerin, Baron Pierre-Narcisse (1774–1833) / Musee de la Revolution Francaise, Vizille, France, Credit: Visual Arts Library / Musee de la Revolution; **74b:** Topfoto.co.uk; **75:** Bridgeman Art Library / *The Meeting of Anthony and Cleopatra* 1747–1750 (fresco), Tiepolo, Giovanni Battista (Giambattista) (1696–1770) / Palazzo Labia, Venice, Italy, Alinari; **76:** Topfoto.co.uk; **77:** Bridgeman Art Library / *The Defeat of Mark Anthony at Actium in 31 BC* (tapestry), Leefdael, Jan van and Strecken, Gerard van der (studio of) / Musee de la Revolution Francaise, Vizille, France, Credit: Visual Arts Library / Musee de la Revolution; **78:** Bridgeman Art Library / Emperor Augustus holding a scepter and thunderbolt, from Herculaneum (stone) (b/w photo), Roman (1st century CE) / Museo Archeologico Nazionale, Naples, Italy / Alinari; **79t:** Alinari Picture Library; **79b:** Sonia Halliday Photographs / M. Montagna; **81t:** Alinari Picture Library; **81b:** Sonia Halliday Photographs; **82:** Corbis / Free Agents Limited; **83:** Bridgeman Art Library / *Virgil Reading the Aeneid to Livia, Octavia and Augustus*, c. 1812 (oil on canvas), Ingres, Jean Auguste Dominique (1780–1867) / Musee des Augustins, Toulouse, France; **84:** Bridgeman Art Library / Sarcophagus of Cornelius Statius depicting scenes from the life of a child (marble), Roman (2nd century CE) / Louvre, Paris, France; **86:** Sonia Halliday Photographs; **87:** AKG Images / Erich Lessing; **88:** Sonia Halliday Photographs / F .H. C. Birch; **89:** Bridgeman Art Library / Shoemaker at work, relief from a Roman sepulcher (stone) (b/w photo), Roman / Cathedral of Notre Dame, Reims, France / Alinari; **90:** AKG Images / Pirozzi; **91:** Sonia Halliday Photographs; **91b:** Bridgeman Art Library / Group of toilet and writing utensils (ivory), Roman (1st century CE) / Fitzwilliam Museum, University of Cambridge, UK; **92:** AKG Images / Erich Lessing; **93:** Corbis / Archivo Icongrafico, S.A.; **94:** Bridgeman Art Library / *A Chat round the Brasero* Phillip, John (1817–1867) / Guildhall Art Gallery, Corporation of London, UK; **95:** Bridgeman Art Library / School scene, from Neumagen, Roman relief panel, 2nd century AD (stone) / Rheinisches Landesmuseum, Trier, Germany, Credit: Bildarchiv Steffens; **96:** Topfoto.co.uk / Ancient Art & Architecture Collection; **97:** AKG Images / Erich Lessing; **98:** Bridgeman Art Library / *Slave Combing a Girl's Hair*, Herculaneum, Third Style (fresco), Roman (1st century CE) / Museo Archeologico Nazionale, Naples, Italy; **100:** Bridgeman Art Library / Sale of a Slave Girl in Rome, 1884 (oil on canvas), Gerome, Jean Leon (1824–1904) / Hermitage, St. Petersburg, Russia; **101:** Bridgeman Art Library / The Ploughman of Arezzo, from Cerveteri / Museo Nazionale di Villa Giulia, Rome, Italy, Alinari; **102:** AKG Images / Erich Lessing; **103:** AKG Images / Erich Lessing; **104t:** Corbis / Bettmann; **104b:** AKG Images / Nimatallah; **105t:** AKG Images / Erich Lessing; **105b:** Corbis / Bettmann; **106:** AKG Images; **108:** AKG Images; **109:** AKG Images; **110:** Andy Chopping/MoLAS; **111t:** Alinari Picture Library; **111b:** AKG Images / Erich Lessing; **112:** Topfoto.co.uk / The British Museum / HIP; **113:** Bridgeman Art Library / *Roman Soldiers Besieging a Town*, plate 23B, class 5 from Part I of *The History of the Nations*, engraved by A. Nani (aquatint), Italian School (19th century) / Private Collection, Credit: The Stapleton Collection; **114:** Bridgeman Art Library / Reconstruction of a Roman legionary from the end of the Republic, 1st century BCE (photo) / Private Collection, Alinari; **115:** Bridgeman Art Library / The Construction of a Roman Camp, detail from Trajan's Column, 2nd century (carved stone), Rome, Italy, Credit: INDEX; **116:** Sonia Halliday Photographs; **119:** Topfoto.co.uk / Charles Walker; **120t:** Bridgeman Art Library / Aerial view of the amphitheater (photo), Roman (2nd century CE) / Arles, France, Giraudon; **121t:** AKG Images / Hillbich; **121b:** Sonia Halliday Photographs; **123b:** AKG Images; **123t:** AKG Images / Erich Lessing.

CONTENTS

JULIUS CAESAR TO THE INVASION OF BRITAIN, 100 BCE–43 CE

100 BCE Expeditions against Mediterranean pirates. Roman citizenship refused to Italians.

88–85 BCE War against Mithridates.

88 BCE Sulla becomes a consul.

86 BCE Sulla captures Athens.

83–82 BCE Sertorius, of Marius Party, urges Spain to oppose Sulla and his political reforms against the Gracchi.

73 BCE Spartacus leads the slaves against Rome.

70 BCE Virgil is born.

67 BCE Pompey destroys Mediterranean pirates.

89 BCE Massacres by Mithridates, Persian King of Pontus, of Italians in Delos and Asia Minor. Greek revolt against Rome. All Italians who ask will be given Roman citizenship.

87 BCE Marius's popular party triumph in Rome. Catullus born.

82 BCE Sulla returns to Rome with his army and crushes the popular party. He becomes dictator.

71 BCE Pompey defeats Spartacus who is assassinated.

65 BCE Birth of Horace the poet. Poetry by Catullus appears.

64 BCE Birth of Livy.

63 BCE Pompey ends war with Mithridates and campaigns in Syria, Judea, Petra and into the Caucasus. Octavius is born. Cataline conspiracy crushed.

60 BCE The first triumvirate. Pompey, Caesar and Crassus.

ITALY SURROUNDED ON THREE SIDES BY THE SEA

59 BCE Caesar a consul.

58 BCE Caesar begins conquest of Gaul.

56 BCE Meeting of triumvirs at Lucca.

55 BCE Caesar in Germany and Britain. Pompey in Spain. Crassus in Syria. Pompey's theater is the first stone-built theater in Rome.

53 BCE Revolt of Vercingetorix in Gaul. Crassus a disaster in Syria and his death at battle of Carrhae. His head is sent back to Rome with his mouth filled with molten gold "as he loved money and gold so much."

51 BCE Caesar writes his *Gallic Wars.*

50 BCE End of Gallic Wars. Gaul as far as the Rhine is a Roman province.

49 BCE Caesar crosses the Rubicon, the frontier between Rome and the north. The power struggle and civil wars begin between him and Pompey.

ABOVE *A modern map of Italy, showing Rome close to the coast.*

OPPOSITE *Modern Rome, showing the sites of the Forum, the Colosseum, Circus Maximus, the Arc of Constantine, the Pantheon and the Appian Way.*

48 BCE Pompey defeated in Egypt and he is murdered there. Caesar with Cleopatra. The library at Alexandria is destroyed.

46 BCE Caesar defeats Pompeians at Thapsus.

45 BCE The last Pompeian defeat at Munda in Spain.

MODERN ROME

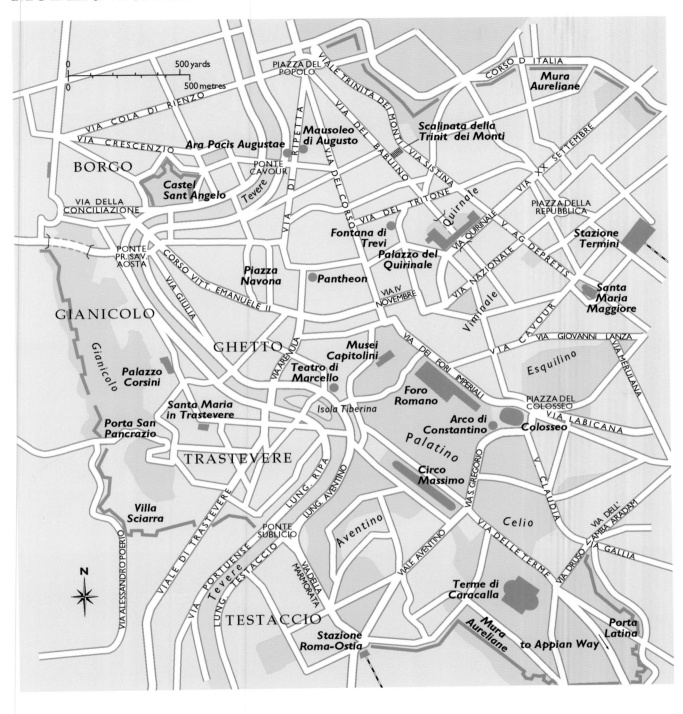

BORGO

Ara Pacis Augustae

Mausoleo di Augusto

Scalinata della Trinit dei Monti

Mura Aureliane

Castel Sant Angelo

PIAZZA DEL POPOLO

PONTE CAVOUR

PIAZZA DELLA REPUBBLICA

Stazione Termini

VIA DELLA CONCILIAZIONE

PONTE PR.SAV. AOSTA

Fontana di Trevi

Palazzo del Quirinale

Quirinale

Santa Maria Maggiore

GIANICOLO

Piazza Navona

Pantheon

GHETTO

Palazzo Corsini

Teatro di Marcello

Musei Capitolini

Esquilino

Santa Maria in Trastevere

Isola Tiberina

Foro Romano

Porta San Pancrazio

Arco di Constantino

Colosseo

PIAZZA DEL COLOSSEO

Palatino

TRASTEVERE

Circo Massimo

Celio

Villa Sciarra

PONTE SUBLICIO

Aventino

Terme di Caracalla

Porta Latina

TESTACCIO

Stazione Roma-Ostia

Mura Aureliane to Appian Way

N

Timeline

44 BCE Caesar assassinated on 15 March—the Ides of March.

43 BCE Second triumvirate—Octavian, Antony and Lepidus. Brutus and Cassius, the leaders of the plot to kill Caesar, move to the east to set up resistance.

42 BCE Brutus and Cassius defeated at Philippi.

32 BCE Agrippa, Octavian's adviser and general, plans Port Julius.

30 BCE Battle of Actium. Octavian and Agrippa crush Antony who flees to Egypt and Cleopatra. They both die and Octavian returns to Rome.

27 BCE Octavian takes the name Augustus and establishes his position as emperor. Cyprus becomes a Roman province.

19 BCE Virgil dies.

16 BCE Tiberius and Drusus (stepsons of Augustus) campaign into Germany.

14 BCE Death of Augustus; Tiberius now emperor.

12 BCE Agrippa dies.

10 BCE Claudius born in Lyons, son of Drusus. Ruled out of the succession as he was crippled at birth.

9 BCE Drusus reaches the Elbe. Varus loses three legions in Germany.

43 CE Conquest of Britain.

41 CE Claudius voted in as emperor by the Praetorian Guard.

INTRODUCTION

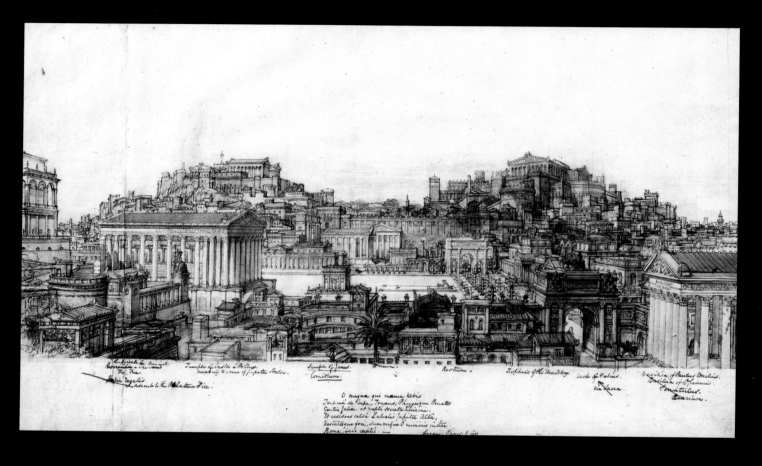

Of arms and the man I sing, who, forced by fate
And proud Juno's never ending hate
Expell'd and exil'd, left the Trojan shore
Long hardships, both by land and sea he bore
And in the doubtful war, before he won
The Latin realm and built the destin'd town;
His banished gods restored to rites divine
And settled sure succession in his line
From whence the race of Alban fathers come,
And the long glories of Majestic Rome.

Virgil, *The Aeneid* **(translated by John Dryden)**

"The Roman Empire was born in fear
and it perished in fear."

John Balsdon, *Rome: The Story of An Empire*

In the Beginning

From the beginning of their history, the Romans had to prove themselves more ruthless than their neighbors, the Etruscans and the Volsci. Rome had to be more cunning, more capable and, if necessary, crueller, for if the city did not defend itself, it would become a victim. The settlement was spread over seven hills, which provided the defensive position for the city as its power grew.

From 753 BCE when the mythical Romulus founded the city as a kingdom, the Romans were determined to control their destiny. It was a destiny driven both by their fear of outsiders and their contempt for the stranger. In their view, anyone not a citizen of Rome was an inferior. It was fear and contempt that drove them to relentlessly conquer land after land and tribe after

tribe to create an empire. While they held down their expanding frontiers they felt secure.

The Longest Empire

The Romans' worst fears were confirmed with the arrival of the Goths at their gates over a 1,000 years later in 410 CE. The city was taken and from that moment the empire crumbled until there remained only fragmentary outposts of a once highly civilized life. It is true, however, that there remain aspects of the Roman Empire that affect our lives today. But what was it that allowed this empire to flower and grow in influence and power for so long? What was the difference between the Roman and the Persian Empire? Or the empire created by Alexander the Great who had reached out and taken Egypt, Syria, Greece, the whole Persian Empire, Palestine and Afghanistan? Alexander was the leader whose exploits Julius Caesar wanted to emulate. Caesar was discovered one day looking at a bust of Alexander and weeping. He explained that although he was nearly twice the age of that roaring warrior he felt he had achieved nothing. Alexander had already conquered the known world by the age of twenty-four.

"What have I done?" Julius Caesar asked. "Look what he did even as a young man."

Maybe the single most important lesson Caesar learned from Alexander was that his power lay in the loyalty and respect of the men he led. Caesar, an ambitious man, felt that time was slipping through his fingers. His opportunity came when he returned in triumph from his wars in Gaul. The Roman Republic began to implode as a result of political chaos in the city.

Expansion and Danger

For 700 years Rome expanded and the city became the great focus for all ambitious men. This may have contributed to its decline for by drawing in the best men from the edges of its empire, Rome diluted the strengths of its component parts.

ABOVE *The Appian Way, near Rome, clearly shows the grooves made by the chariot wheels.*

What is left of the physical evidence of the empire inside the modern city of Rome? The skeletons of some of the empire's great buildings still exist, and they give us an idea of its important legacy. Consider three of the surviving monuments: the Appian Way, the Forum and the Colosseum. The Appian Way leads directly into the city and still exists 2,000 years after its construction. It was constructed to link with military roads in the east and west of the empire and join Spain and Macedonia and Asia. It provides a reminder of the power of the Roman Army, which marched along its length to provide frontier security for Rome.

The Roman Forum, with its elegant columns and spaces, was copied in every major city in the empire as a place in which debate, ideas and the creation of the rule of law provided the focus for the city. It was in the Forum that Romans discussed the issues of the day and it was from here that decisions were transmitted to distant parts of the empire. The Forum was a place where only the rich and the influential were heard, the voice of the ordinary man was not often heard in debate. It was on the steps of the Forum that the ambitions of one man to become dictator of the city ended under the assassin's knife. On March 15, 44 BCE Julius Caesar met his death here. The columns and stones are a reminder that Romans believed in political discussion and the rule of law. When those began to weaken the empire began to crumble.

The Colosseum is the most powerful symbol of late Rome, the empire, its freeborn citizens and the power of the mob. In this vast amphitheater, the sand was soaked in the blood of innocents, prisoners of war, criminals, slaves and gladiators. Here ritualized slaughter was carried out, beloved of the mob and also of many of the later emperors and their acolytes. Ruinously expensive mock games, battles and individual gladiatorial contests all had one end—death. The Colosseum was a place of horror. It was a place where violence, lack of honor and cruel disinterest in their fellow men became the watchword of the Romans. It was here that the moral feebleness of the rulers and the mob they feared was made public and was approved. It is possible to conclude that in the sand of the Colosseum the mighty empire truly fell.

Yet before it fell, the Roman Empire displayed some strengths that were never lost. Why did it grow and why did it fall? Who were the main players in the story of Rome? What aspects of the Roman Empire do we value even now? *Rome* will answer these questions.

It is not just the villas, public buildings, aqueducts, theaters, roads, temples and bridges that demonstrate the empire that was Rome. It was so much more. In time these buildings will vanish as Roman cities have already been covered by desert sands in North Africa, Persia, Jordan and Syria. The answer does not lie in the might of the Roman Army, although that was considerable. There have been other armies before and since with the same ruthlessness and the same powerful leadership. It is not even the study of men such as Julius Caesar, Augustus, Pliny, Cicero, Virgil, Nero, Claudius or even Spartacus that really touches the core of the question, although they are important to our understanding of the history of Rome.

Beyond buildings, leaders and roads there rests the powerful matter of connections across frontiers and communication between cities. The language of Rome became the lingua franca of Europe for 1,000 years after the empire fell, and the code of laws that the ancient Romans introduced have been the bedrock of the legal systems over much of the world ever since. It is to the continuity of ideas of justice and the law, which held together the Roman Empire, that we still owe so much.

The Roman Empire was defined by the city and the citizens—practical, cool and determined people whose leaders believed that those beyond their borders were savages or outsiders who were certainly unworthy of Roman citizenship. This changed as the empire expanded. From Mesopotamia to the northern borders of Britain, from Spain to the dark forests of Germany, from North Africa to Macedonia, into Asia and through Palestine and the edge of the Arabian sands. Into Egypt, along the Euphrates, along the wall Hadrian built in the north of England. This was the Empire.

Fate

Rome's prosperity appeared to be unending. It was not. As the Greek-Alexandrian poet Constantine Cavafy (1863–1933) wrote:

> *The Barbarians will arrive today.*
> *When the Barbarians come they'll*
> *make the laws...*
>
> *Some people have arrived from the Frontier;*
> *They said there are no Barbarians any more.*
> *What will become of us without Barbarians?*

The barbarians eventually arrived at the gates of Rome. It was the end of glory. But first came great men and great deeds—heroes and villains, kind men and cruel, and here lies the fear at the end of it all. Here is *Rome*.

BELOW *A view over the Roman Forum also showing the Temple of Vesta, the Arch of Titus and the Temple of Castor and Pollux.*

From Myth to Empire

EVERY MAJOR CITY has its physical foundations buried in time and there are almost always myths concerning its historical foundations buried too. Rome is not unusual in this respect. One of the myths concerns the naming of the city. The other, a more literary retelling of the city's origins, connects the foundation of Rome with one of the heroes of the siege of Troy. This story is the core of *The Aeneid*, an epic poem, which was written by the Latin poet Virgil (70–19 BCE) for Augustus (27 BCE–14 CE), the first emperor of Rome. The intent was to create a connection between Augustus and Romulus, the mythical founder of the city, and in doing so make a connection between the first emperor and the gods. Along with many other myths, *The Aeneid* provides a vivid picture of the heroes who created the city of Rome.

OPPOSITE *A 1,700-year-old mosaic from Isurium Brigantum, a Roman town established in present-day North Yorkshire, England.*

The Myth—Aeneas, Romulus and the Beginning of Rome

The Aeneid takes as its hero Aeneas, a Trojan prince and the son of the Greek goddess Aphrodite. At the end of the ten-year siege of Troy, Aeneas's wife, Creusa, a daughter of King Priam of Troy, urged him to leave the city, which was being sacked by the Greeks. Creusa told her husband that his destiny was to found a great city. Although he loved her he knew he had to obey his fate. Creusa remained in the burning city while Aeneas fled, accompanied by his father, Anchises, and son, Ascanius.

Aeneas wandered for many years until he came to the coast of Latium. Eventually, he married Lavinia, the daughter of the local king, Latinus, and established himself in the city of Lavinium. Upon Aeneas's death, Ascanius founded the city of Alba. The descendants of Aeneas had ruled this region for 300 years when Numitor was overthrown by his cruel and overambitious brother Amulius. Numitor's sons were murdered and his daughter, Rhea, forced to remain a virgin. However, she gave birth to twin sons, Romulus and Remus, having been visited by Mars, the god of war.

A furious Amulius had the twins thrown into the River Tiber, but the boys survived, suckled by a wolf and then reared by a shepherd. Eventually the twins learned their secret, killed Amulius and restored the throne of Alba to their grandfather. The twins decided to found a city of their own nearby. Romulus won the honor of naming it, having witnessed a good omen when he saw 12 vultures circling Mount Palatine—Remus only saw six. Jealous at his brother's good fortune, Remus jumped over the city walls that Romulus was building, mocking their height. This infuriated Romulus so much that he picked up his sword and killed his twin. So Rome—in myth at least—was founded in 753 BCE.

The Rape of the Sabine Women

Romulus had an army of men to populate his city, but he had no women for them. To provide wives for his warriors, he invited his neighbors, the Sabines, to a festival and promptly carried off their daughters. As a result the Romans and the Sabines went to war. The Sabines entered Rome through the treachery of Tarpeia, daughter of the Roman commander, who said that she would allow the Sabines in to the city if they would give her all that they wore on their left hands. However, the Sabines were honorable men and furious that such an act of betrayal had led to their victory. Instead of giving Tarpeia the gold rings and bracelets that they wore on their left arms, they threw their heavy shields on her, crushing her to death. From this moment the Romans and the Sabines lived in peace together. Another version of the same myth ends with the Sabine women telling their fathers that they were content to be the wives of Roman warriors. Romulus extended his immediate territory and ensured the safety of his city, which he ruled for nearly 40 years. Upon his death, he was taken to heaven by his father, Mars.

A City at War

Defense and trade were the keys to the geographical position of Rome. Both had a bearing on the growth and future of the empire of which Rome was the hub. The city was built on the south bank of the River Tiber on a group of seven easily defended hilltops. The small port of Ostia, which was downstream from the fortified city, soon came under the control of Rome and became the focus for all trading activity in the immediate area.

OPPOSITE *Aeneas, before escaping from the burning city of Troy with his lame father, Anchises, and his son, Ascanius. His wife, Creusa, offers him the figures of the household gods.*

LEFT *The remains of the Roman port of Ostia situated a few miles along the River Tiber.*

Once it was united as one settlement, the city was a perfect base from which to wage war on local tribes and to control the surrounding lands. It may be that the incursion by the Sabines was enough to cause concern about the security of the Roman frontier, for it became the perpetual fear of successive rulers.

From 753 to 509 BCE Rome was at war with its other neighbors, as it struggled to consolidate its position. It is likely that the mysterious Etruscans (see panel), who ruled an area that stretched from the River Po to Campania, were in control of Rome from about 600 BCE. The legendary monarchs of the city, among them the last king, Tarquinius Superbus (534–510 BCE), were probably Etruscan (see pages 29 and 31). In 510 BCE, the Romans expelled this foreign king and with him the idea of "kingship." Fundamental to the growth of the city, and its emerging empire, was the refusal of its inhabitants to accept that one man should rule over them.

The Expansion of Rome, 509–204 BCE

Following the overthrow of the monarchy, Rome became a republic (see pages 31–32), which meant that its citizens had a part to play in the city's government and its expanding territories.

The Etruscans continued to hold land to the north of the city. The Greeks, who had colonized various city states along the southern coast of Italy and the island of Sicily, for example, Syracuse, were confident that they would remain independent of this emergent power. However, other tribes threatened the security of Rome.

The Roman Republic relied on the citizens' army in which every man was expected to give service to the state if called on. Its officers came from the ruling class—the patricians—whose sons were trained from childhood to lead the military against any threat to the city. However, some of Rome's adversaries were able to put better-trained and bigger armies into the field.

In 463 BCE the warlike tribes of the Volsci and the Aequi came within 3 miles (five km) of the gates of Rome. At the same time Rome lost control of the colonies of citizens it had placed in the towns that it had conquered during the previous generation (see panel, page 19). However, by 418 BCE Rome had taken back all the territory seized by the Aequi to the east thus securing communication with its allies. At the same time Roman troops were also consolidating their positions in the south, undertaking a rapid and bold advance through Volscian-held land to the town of Tarracina, which the Romans took and plundered. Rome took back colonies it had lost to the south and east and forged new alliances to hold the plain of Labium and the strongholds that dominated the surrounding hill country. Former allies of Rome that had rebelled were forced to sue for peace—some were destroyed by a vengeful Roman army.

While the Romans were consolidating their position in the south and east, the Etruscans, their most dangerous enemy at this point, were under threat from the Gauls in the north and the Greeks

THE ETRUSCANS

The Etruscans, who were centerd in Erturia (modern Tuscany), were not Latin by race and it is believed that they came into northern Italy from Asia Minor. They left few signs of their civilization apart from some dramatic pottery figurines and equally strong wall paintings. Perhaps their greatest contribution to Rome was architectural. They created buildings using both the arch and the vault. They also gave the Romans the idea of gladiatorial combat for entertainment and the belief that it was possible to divine the wishes of the gods from studying animals.

BELOW *An Etruscan fresco showing a lively banquet scene. It is a tomb painting from the first half of the fifth century BCE.*

in the south. The immense power of the Etruscans was sapped by these pressures. It was time for Rome to try to secure her northern borders, which were under the control of the Etruscans. A newly confident Rome took the opportunity to defeat the southern Etruscan cities. The primary Etruscan settlement in the region was Veii, its vast riches made it worthy of capture, and it was only about 12 miles (19 km) northwest of Rome. The main ally of Veii was a Latin town, Fidenae, that was situated on the south bank of the Tiber just five miles (eight km) from Rome. The Romans captured Fidenae in 428 BCE and totally destroyed it. Under Marcus Furius Camillus, Roman forces beseiged Veii. For Camillus to keep the siege of Veii in place, his army had to remain under arms for months. As a consequence of this, Roman soldiers were paid for the first time, as they were no longer just an army of citizens brought together during the summer fighting season. As

ROMAN COLONIES

The settlement of Roman families in captured territory was a common policy of the Romans to ensure that each city had within it a garrison that was entirely controlled from Rome. It meant, for example, that the city states captured along the coast would always be available to Roman vessels and would provide secure headquarters for further military expansion. Colonies like these grew throughout the Roman Empire as it expanded.

Veii fell in 396 BCE, the Gauls broke through into Etruscan lands in the north. The Etruscans no longer posed an imminent threat to Rome.

However, there was now a much more dangerous adversary to contend with. The Gauls of the north, who populated a region running north of the Po to the Alps that was known as Cisalpine Gaul, were regarded as barbarians. These men were powerful and well-organized warriors.

BELOW *A sixteenth-century engraved map of the city of Rome. The Tiber runs through the city. Note the long defensive wall that leads into the foothills.*

When the Romans turned to confront the Gauls at the Battle of Allia in 390 BCE, their army was routed by their much better organized and more experienced adversaries. This left Rome open for the taking. The Gauls needed no invitation. They stormed into the city and pillaged it before withdrawing with their loot.

Rome now appeared to be at the mercy of all those it had defeated over the years. The army fell into disarray and was now attacked by the Volsci, the Aequi, the Etruscans and even by some of its Latin allies. The city survived this disaster because its position was still strongly fortified and because of the leadership skills of Camillus. He took the battered and dispirited army, rebuilt its confidence and destroyed the Volsci and the Aequi in the 380s. Then, turning rapidly north he took back all that the Etruscans had secured.

Rome began to perceive itself as capable of forcing all her Italian enemies into submission. Even the powerful Gauls, who continued to invade

from time to time, were pushed back across the River Po. In 358 BCE the Romans reestablished their links with their Latin allies. Now Rome was in a position to take on the remaining threats to its security, but first it built new alliances with the tribes living on the coastal plain of the Adriatic Sea. These tough warriors were willing to fight alongside the Roman army against the Samnites—a common enemy and a warlike tribe that ranged throughout the Apennines, the range of mountains looming over Campania. The Romans captured Gavius Pontus, a Samnite leader whom they executed.

In 293 BCE the Samnites finally capitulated, although they never abandoned their hatred for Rome. In a last push for security on the mainland of Italy, Rome confronted Greek city states such as Tarentum (modern Taranto), a rich city that owed its wealth to its harbor and its traders.

When Tarentum attacked one of Rome's allies, the Thurii, and also took and sold into slavery the

BELOW *Rome takes the island of Sicily during the Punic Wars against Carthage. An oil painting by Jacopo Ripanda.*

PYRRHUS OF EPIRUS

Pyrrhus, the king of Epirus, was a warlike leader whose experience was garnered as a commander in major wars after the death of his cousin Alexander the Great. He had great confidence in his ability to defeat the Roman upstarts. In 280 BCE Pyrrhus landed at Tarentum in command of an army of professional soldiers. He had 20,000 infantry and 5,000 cavalry, including 20 war elephants. Despite having some semblance of a professional army, Rome was still heavily reliant on amateur militia and, all other things being equal, no such army can defeat professionals.

RIGHT *The battle of Heraclea (280 BCE) when King Pyrrhus of Epirus defeated the Romans. Note the war elephants that caused havoc among the Roman army. Engraving c. 1630.*

BELOW *A bust of Pyrrhus, the king of Epirus, who led the forces of Tarentum against the Romans.*

Pyrrhus was victorious in battle at Heraclea, but lost 4,000 men. In 281 BCE he sent a diplomat, Cineas, to Rome to sue for peace. Cineas was told bluntly by the blind senator Appius Claudius to leave the city, as Rome would never negotiate with Pyrrhus while he stayed on Italian soil.

The Roman army used hit-and-run tactics against Pyrrhus's troops. They refused to stand and fight a pitched battle and harried the opposing army on its flanks, its front and its rear. Pyrrhus won a battle at Ausculum in 279 BCE but again lost many men. This time he managed to arrange an armistice.

The military adventurer in Pyrrhus led him to turn aside from the battle against Rome and to attack the Carthaginians in Sicily. But in 275 BCE he returned to attack the Romans at Beneventum where his army was so heavily defeated that he abandoned the campaign and his allies. He died in Argos three years later in a street battle.

It is said that as he left Italy Pyrrhus prophesied "How fair a battlefield I am leaving in Sicily for the Romans and the Carthaginians."

crews of a Roman squadron of ten ships, war was inevitable. Rome laid waste to the area around the city and the Democrat government of Tarentum called on Pyrrhus of Epirus (319–272 BCE) for help (see panel).

The Punic Wars

Carthage, a city state that centered on modern Tunis, was always a threat to Roman ambition and already had an empire that stretched along the North African coastline, through the southern Mediterranean and up into Spain. It was a city with a long history and a powerful past. Carthage controlled overland trade in North Africa and sea trade from the Atlantic into the western Mediterranean.

Carthage was ruled by a "Committee of 100" whose influence was supreme. The city seemed to be invulnerable. Yet the self-interest and self-seeking of the ruling clique would cause the downfall of the wealth and influence of Carthage. Corruption, greed and the lust for power meant that the military was never allowed to expand beyond the control of the city's oligarchy. They feared their own generals would turn on them and so they refused them enough funds or the freedom to capitalize on their military successes.

Rome had to defeat the Carthaginian Empire if it was to take its position as a dominant power in the known world. The interests of the cities were too closely connected for their empires to coexist and three wars, known as the Punic Wars, were fought between the two powers for supremacy in the Mediterranean. The First Punic War lasted from 264 to 241 BCE; the Second Punic War began in 218 BCE and ended in 201 BCE; and the Third Punic War ran from 149 to 146 BCE.

When the two states came into conflict it was, inevitably, over the ownership of the islands off southern Italy, among them Sicily and Corsica, which were under the heel of Carthage. The Romans invaded Messana (modern Messina) in Sicily. Then, in 263 BCE the Carthaginians concentrated a force in the area of Agrigentum. The Romans besieged their enemy with 100,000 men. Both sides suffered from the plague and hunger, and after seven months the Carthaginians

cut their way out of the city and abandoned it to the Romans who had lost as many as 30,000 men. In 259 BCE Carthage ceded Corsica to Rome. Roman forces attempted to take the war to the African mainland, but were beaten back.

Carthaginian quinqueremes (galleys) held the power at sea. The Romans, who were not experienced in naval conflict, built a navy to take the war beyond Italy, which would mean taking on the powerful Carthaginian fleet. In order to gain an advantage at sea the Romans invented the corvus, an ingenious 36-foot (12-meter) gangway the width of two men with a sharp spike on its underside that was slung from the mast of a ship. When two ships engaged, the Romans lowered the corvus and locked ships together while their soldiers poured across the gangway into the enemy vessel.

Under Marcus Atilius Regulus, the Romans won a decisive sea battle and destroyed 36

Carthaginian ships. The way to Africa was open. There they were successful at first and won battle after battle on the open plains. They took 20,000 slaves during this campaign.

Rome proposed impossible demands for a peace settlement, which left the Carthaginians in such despair that they imported Xanthippus, a Spartan soldier of fortune who had fought in the armies of Alexander the Great. He turned the fortunes of the Carthaginians at Clupea on the coast, where the Romans were trampled under fearsome war elephants and Regulus was captured. The Romans had ceased to be a danger to Carthage on African soil by 255 BCE.

Fortunes swung back and forth at sea, but in 249 BCE, toward the end of the period of naval battles, the Carthaginian fleet trapped the Romans between the shore and their vast and experienced fleet. The Romans lost all but 30 of their 210 ships; 20,000 prisoners were taken, and then a second force was swept away in a storm. The First Punic War came to its natural end with both Carthage and Rome

having suffered grievous losses. They had fought themselves to a standstill and from 241 to 218 BCE the two cities stood down in what seemed to be an armed truce.

The Mighty Hannibal

The Second Punic War was a long-drawn-out campaign. The battles were fought in Spain and through the Alps and down into Italy. For much of the time the Romans experienced the bitterness of defeat after defeat at the hands of Hannibal (247–182 BCE).

Hannibal had come into his own and the centralized power in Rome was not able to respond to the speed and ingenuity of this remarkable Carthaginian general. He was beginning a career that would confirm him as the greatest and most innovative opponent the Roman army had yet confronted. In fighting against him the Romans learned lessons that enabled them to forge an invincible army in the future.

Hannibal made Cartagena the center of Carthaginian power in Spain. This was a break for independence from his political masters in Carthage. He began to push north as Rome tried to use proxies such as the Saguntine tribe to harass him. A messenger was sent to Hannibal to demand reparation for the damage done so far. The Roman was told there was no chance of that. It was either war or peace.

It was war. Hannibal made his first move very quickly indeed. The Romans sent their most powerful general, Publius Cornelius Scipio (236–183 BCE) to intercept him, but Hannibal had already crossed the Pyrenees and was preparing to cross the River Rhone. It is a truth that a good soldier learns most from a sound defeat. The Romans were about to experience it. The battles in Italy that led to the Battle of Cannae in 216 BCE were lessons in quick-thinking,

LEFT *A bust of the great Carthaginian general Hannibal (247–182 BCE).*

swift movement and brilliant tactics, which no Roman general would ever forget. By the time Hannibal emerged from the Pyrenees he had lost 40,000 infantrymen and 3,000 cavalry. It was September and snow was falling when Hannibal began to cross the Alps. Avalanches and hostile tribes were a constant danger but Hannibal marched on. In the ice and cold the cavalry suffered badly and the infantry did not have an easy time. He lost many more men and horses by the time he descended from the mountains.

Hannibal always moved like lightning and this time was no different. He gave his men a few days' rest and then went into battle. At the Battle of Ticinus in 218 BCE Scipio thought his troops could easily beat an army that had just fought its way through avalanches and attacks by local tribesmen. Scipio was wrong. His army was defeated, he was wounded and had to fall back on the River Po where he destroyed the bridges and retreated to Trebia.

Scipio was now joined by Publius Sempronius, who had been sent with reinforcements. It was a decision driven by politics rather than prudent strategy. Sempronius had no experience of command in battle. Scipio understood war and insisted that their position, defended by the River Trebia, was secure. But Sempronius was determined to attack and gain the credit for defeating Hannibal. Confronting Hannibal at Trebia, Sempronius could not have realized how eager Hannibal was for them to attack him.

On a bleak December morning the Romans attacked what Sempronius believed was a weakened Carthaginian army. They came through the mists, crossed the icy stream and instead of a battle-weary and demoralized force they confronted a well-fed and rested Carthaginian force perfectly deployed for the battle. Hannibal wanted to fight. The Romans were yet again defeated.

At this moment the Romans chose yet again to replace their commander. Gaius Flaminius was a man whose policy had always been to get the enemy on the run and keep him on the run. This was all very well if the enemy was a horde of unruly barbarians, but in Hannibal he was facing one of the greatest tacticians of all time. Hannibal already knew from his intelligence sources that his opponent was given to rashness.

Hannibal moved into Etruria and Flaminius, and overeager, did not see the trap that was being prepared for him. It was sprung in 216 BCE by Lake Trasimene. Hemmed in by mountains, on the small plain close to the lake, the Carthaginian army was drawn up on a slight rise. Hannibal secretly sent his cavalry to the end of the pass with orders to close it as soon as Flaminius had led his army towards the plain and the lake.

The Romans came out of a light mist and found the Carthaginian main army on rising ground ahead of them. Its flanks were exposed to the enemy hidden in the mountains. As soon as the last cohort passed the entrance to the pass, they were attacked from the rear by Carthaginian cavalry. The Romans were annihilated. The cavalry sent as reinforcements were also surprised and slaughtered. The next day the Romans were forced to surrender after Flaminius died on the battlefield. It was a disaster for the Roman army.

The Battle at Cannae came too soon for those lessons to have been absorbed.

Despite his victories, Hannibal knew that he had been weakened by these battles. He also

OPPOSITE *Hannibal and his army with ox-drawn baggage carts are led through a mountain pass during the Second Punic War.*

BELOW *The Romans under Flaminius and the Carthaginian army led by Hannibal fighting at Lake Trasimene (Spring 216 BCE).*

realized that his lines of communication were overstretched and that he was not powerful enough to take Rome by direct assault. But he was happy to harry and to destroy the defensive confederacy that the Romans had built around their city. He was also one of the first propagandists in war. He kept his Roman prisoners under harsh conditions, but sent home those Italian prisoners who lived without the benefit of Roman citizenship.

Hannibal headed into Apulia and was now a very potent threat to Rome. The army the Romans now put together to confront Hannibal was made up of 40,000 men in all. Again command was divided, this time between Gaius Terentius Varro, who had no experience of battle, and Aemillius Paullus, a man of experience who was unpopular. The two Roman commanders compounded the problems of a split command by agreeing to hold power on alternate days!

The Battle of Cannae was fought on an open plain that favored those on horseback and as Hannibal had 10,000 cavalrymen he had the advantage there. On the other hand, his infantry was half that of the Romans. Cavalry was the key and any experienced general would have made suitable changes in the disposition of his men if faced by such a superior force of horsemen. Varro did not have the experience and determined to fight on an open front line.

The cavalry of both sides was drawn up on the wings in the traditional formation with the heavy infantry in the center and the faster and more lightly armed infantry to the front. Hannibal's instructions were to draw the Roman troops deep into the center. This was a dangerous maneuver, as Hannibal relied on his troops retreating slowly but still holding the Romans.

The Carthaginian troops retreated to an agreed point and the Romans believed they had victory in their hands. Then the Gauls and the Spanish, fighting for Carthage, peeled off to the flanks and revealed a new center line of Numidian forces.

While the Romans tried to deal with this new force, the Gauls and the Spanish regrouped and then fell onto the Roman flanks. These were vulnerable because a close formation like a Roman column is only truly effective if it can break the ranks of the enemy. Hannibal had made them believe they were about to do just that. The Romans were surrounded as Hannibal turned his cavalry loose on the Roman rear. The defeat

became a massacre. It is said that 50,000 died and 10,000 were taken prisoner. No more than 10,000 men escaped the killing field at Cannae. One of them was Varro.

In other circumstances and against another enemy this would have destroyed the Roman Empire. But the Romans were proud, unbowed, ambitious and determined. They would learn the lessons Hannibal taught them.

It would take 29 years for the Romans to dislodge Hannibal and drive him back through Spain and to Carthage. It would take another five years to pursue him from Carthage, whose rulers abandoned him. When he took refuge with Prusias, King of Bithynia, he was 64 years old. He inspired such fear that the Romans demanded he be surrendered to them. Hannibal knew it was the end. He also knew that he might expect a degrading death and he poisoned himself in 182 BCE. So died the greatest tactician the Romans ever confronted.

The Third Punic War ended with Carthage reduced to rubble and ploughed into the earth. Its people were sent into slavery and Rome was triumphant. Carthage was no longer a potent threat and from this moment the Romans were in charge of their own destiny. Rome controlled the long peninsula from the Po in the north to Sicily in the south. But how was this emerging empire to be ruled?

ABOVE *The end of Carthage. The city is burned to the ground and its whole population enslaved or slaughtered. Copper engraving by Matthaus Merian (1593–1650).*

OPPOSITE *The Battle of Cannae (August 216 BCE) from an illuminated manuscript by Jean Fouquet (c. 1415/20–1477/81).*

Ruling Rome

CHAPTER II

THERE WERE three phases in the government of Rome:

The Kingdom: 753–509 BCE

The Republic: 509–31 BCE

The Empire: 27 BCE–476 CE

For the first 38 years from its foundation, the mythical kingdom of Rome was ruled by Romulus (see page 17). As founder, designer and builder of the city he exercised total control over its government. When Romulus died he was succeeded by Pompilius, who was said to have given the Romans their law and their religion. His successors consolidated the security of the city.

It was usual for the king to take advice from a council of elders, which limited his power. The king's position was not hereditary, instead he was elected by a committee of 300 members of the ruling patrician class—the original Senate. The members of this class were representatives of the various families and clans within the city. In matters of state, the king referred to the Senate and no change in law was valid without its consent.

In addition to the Senate there was what might be termed a Supreme Court. The men of this court had to agree with the king's election, and were able to exercise the right of pardon if the king allowed a prisoner to appeal against sentence of death. As they directly represented the ten tribes who made up the citizens of Rome, they voted in blocks and not as individuals. ❧

OPPOSITE *A marble bas-relief of a gathering of Roman senators.*

The plebeian class had no power and had to accept what was handed down by the patricians, who had the ear of the king. This began to change when Servius Tullius, the legendary sixth king of Rome, came to the throne in about 578 BCE. Tullius was born into the plebeian class but married the daughter of the fourth king, Tarquinius Priscius. He was determined that the representation of the people should be based on property and not on accident of birth and he founded the *Comitia Centuriata*, an assembly of Roman citizens that included the plebeians. The changes he instigated precipitated a revolt by the patrician families, who felt that their power was threatened.

Tullius was eventually murdered. The conduct of the remaining kings of Rome led to the monarchy's fall. Tarquinius Superbus, the last king, ruled as a tyrant. His pride and cruelty, and that of his sons, caused his downfall. According to legend, a virtuous Roman lady named Lucretia was violated by the son of Tarquinius. She took the ultimate revenge, gathering her relatives around her and stabbing herself. Her family were forced to avenge her. The people of Rome rose against the king and his family, who had so abused their power, and they were forced to flee from Rome. It was the end of the monarchy.

Family

Other institutions had also been growing in importance during the period of Roman kings. Family and the bonds of blood relationships were always powerful influences on the development of law and, in particular, of Roman life. In public matters a son might be a magistrate and have power over his father in this domain, but this was never the case within the family itself. The head of a family had absolute power over the private conduct of all members of his clan.

But there was always a sense of loyalty to the state, something that can be exemplified by the actions of a magistrate named Brutus. He had to pronounce sentence on several patricians, including two of his own sons, who were accused of conspiring to bring back the tyrannical Tarquinius. The charge was treason and the sentence was laid down by law. Brutus sentenced his own two sons to death. It was his duty as a citizen of Rome. His paternal feelings had to be set aside for the good and honor of the state.

The legendary kingdom of Rome lasted for 244 years. The city now faced a period of great institutional and constitutional change.

The Republic, 509–531 BCE

A key development at the start of the Republic was that some of the regal power was passed to two annually elected officials called consuls. At first the only block to a consul's power was that wielded by the other consul who could act as a check on any excessive demands or laws suggested by the other. Consuls were exclusively chosen from the ranks of the patricians, although this changed.

In about 494 BCE the patricians agreed to the creation of a plebeian magistracy. At first this collegium of magistrates consisted of two men, called tribunes, but this was later expanded to five. They had great power, as they could veto the decisions of other magistrates and were themselves untouchable. Their defense of the interests of the plebeian classes were almost sacred and they were a powerful force throughout the period of the Republic.

The patricians attempted to keep control of the power in the state but the plebeians became organized and determined that the right to power as a result solely of land ownership and wealth was not conducive to equity before the law. The plebeians were determined to acquire the right to be elected as consuls despite the opposition

OPPOSITE *In this sixteenth-century oil painting by Paolo Veronese (1528–1588), the virtuous Roman lady Lucretia dies honorably by her own hand.*

BELOW *A procession of senators (and their wives) from a marble altar frieze of the ninth century BCE that commemorates the return of Augustus from the Spanish Campaigns.*

of the patricians. The plebeians got what they demanded only by resorting to threats to secede from the state. As a result of their final threat in 287 BCE they created a council of plebeians, which could make decisions with the force of law. It is from this institution that we have the word "plebiscite."

The power struggle between the plebeians and the patricians continued. In 133 BCE there was severe disruption as a result of the reforms proposed by Gracchus (see panel) who requested the fair distribution of land to war veterans. This unrest resulted in armed skirmishes that bordered on civil war, short-lived dictatorships and

temporary truces. Rome's military and diplomatic expansion of power around the Mediterranean also changed the balance of power. Outside the city, corruption was rife and military commanders needed only the support of the army to take whatever they wanted from the areas they controlled. Commanding an army in one of the provinces amounted to permission to print money.

Gracchus had made a genuine attempt to solve the problems of poverty in rural areas and massive unemployment in the city, but his solutions did nothing but increase the anger of the people, which was whipped up by interested parties among the patrician landowners.

The Senatorial Party (also known as the Optimate Party) was apparently in control of the government. Most members of this group were ex-magistrates. Sulla (see panel, page 34) was a powerful member of this group. The equestrian order, also known as the knights, was next in the pecking order. These wealthy men were not involved in government, but used their money to bring them the influence they desired. Cicero, the orator, was a powerful voice within this class.

The Democrat Party took its strength from the mob. Julius Caesar (see page 39) was its main supporter for a time. He disliked and mistrusted the power wielded by the Senate and wanted to extend Roman privileges to new classes of citizens of the empire. There was also the ultra-conservative Cataline party whose interests lay in preserving the old Roman order.

The continually expanding empire was now ruled from the center by a group of men who were unable to control the threat posed by victorious regional commanders with potentially dangerous armies at their disposal. In 71 BCE, an army of slaves rebelled, led by Spartacus (see page 103). The fact that it was not quickly crushed by the Senate was seen as a sign of the inherent weakness of these legislators.

The Republic came to an end with the Civil Wars. Like all such conflicts, the Roman Civil Wars (see chapters four and six) were divisive, cruel and very bitterly fought. They resulted in the return of rule by one man, initially Julius Caesar. Whatever its divisions the Republic had left a system of lawgiving that was much more egalitarian than it had been at the end of the Kingdom. The consuls were obliged to take heed of their own experience and also to abide by the decisions of committees of wise men and of experienced legislators.

GRACCHUS

Gaius Gracchus was born to a noble family in 154 BCE. He was present at the siege of Carthage in 134 BCE and was appointed to carry out the agrarian reforms of his brother, Tiberius. He became a quaestor (government officer) in 126 BCE and tribune two years later. In 123 BCE he was reelected as a tribune and he continued his reformist policies. He attacked the Senate's privileges, and provided for the distribution of wheat at cheap prices. He also created the structure for the foundation of Roman colonies at Tarentum and Carthage. Gracchus also limited military service, and initiated public works to occupy the unemployed. He ensured that the equestrian class could set and collect taxes in the newly acquired provinces in Asia where they also had control of criminal juries. He suggested that all Italians should be given Roman citizenship, but this provoked the Senate to outlaw him. He fled Rome but was captured and killed with 3,000 of his supporters.

BELOW *The great political leader Gaius Sempronius Gracchus addresses the people.*

The Empire

The Roman Empire began after the Second Civil War had ended (see page 76). Octavian became the Emperor Augustus and it was on his skill, cunning, strength and control of the army and of the divided people of Rome that lay the only chance for their future as an empire.

Rule by one man was the pragmatic answer to the pressing need for sustained control of the center, of the provinces and of the frontiers. Once tasted, such complete power is impossible to give up without a struggle. The emperors who followed Augustus gradually lost their grip on all except their own pleasures and their own personal ambitions. There was no room for loyalty in a court where cruel intrigue and ruthless ambition was the watchword. In this situation lay the danger for Rome. By removing all need for loyalty, by crushing all dissent, by presiding over the erosion of a moral basis for the succession and finally by relying on the army the emperors slowly lost the

ABOVE *A marble bas-relief of senators from the arch of Trajan, Benevento.*

LEFT *A marble portrait bust of Gaius Julius Caesar (100–144 BCE), Roman statesman and general.*

SULLA

Lucius Cornelius Sulla was born in 138 BCE, the son of a poor patrician family. He became quaestor to the senator, Marius, in 107 BCE, praetor in 93 BCE and governor of the province of Cilicia. At age 50 he was made a consul after taking charge of the war against Mithridates in Persia. This appointment was opposed by the Democrat Party, which was led by Marius, who was threatened by the political ambitions of his former protégé. Sulla marched on Rome with his army and put Marius to flight. Sulla returned to the east and eventually crushed the King of Pontus and returned to Rome where Marius was again in power. Sulla crushed his party and became sole master of Rome. He threw out all of Marius's reforms of the Senate, took the power away from popular public institutions and massacred many of his opponents. He resigned in 79 BCE and died peacefully in Puteoli a year later.

LEFT *Lucius Sulla (138–178 BCE), the Roman consul and general. A ruthless leader and dictator of Rome.*

BELOW *Marble bust of Augustus the first Emperor c. 20 CE.*

people and once that happened, the empire was finally lost.

It was 200 years before the Roman Empire ceased its expansion and began, as all empires eventually must, to decline and to fade. Carthage had once seemed invincible and yet it lay under the sand and no life stirred there. The miracle of Rome is that it grew and survived for so many years. The period of empire that began with Augustus, survived as long as it did because, despite power being held by a single individual, it was built on the bedrock of civil, military and political systems that had evolved from the Kingdom through to the Republic.

THE OFFICES OF ROME

AEDILES

Aediles took on the duties of police magistrates and the maintenance of all the public works in Rome. This, in time, led to them having to pay the costs of the city's games. It was an arduous duty and men in this position were open to bribery and corruption as the financial demands on the position grew greater.

CONSUL

A consul was the highest form of magistrate during the period of the Roman Republic. Two consuls with equal power were elected annually. A consul could be opposed by his fellow consul or by the tribunes (see below). Initially both consuls were patricians, but this changed in 367 BCE when it was decided that one should also be plebeian. After Augustus came to power, the consuls lost a great deal of their influence.

EQUESTRIANS/KNIGHTS

During the period of the Roman monarchy, the equestrians were men capable of bringing horses to the battlefield. After the reforms begun by the Gracchus brothers, they became a political party formed from a commercial and trading class. They were free to create banks, public works departments and trading houses. During the period of the emperors, knights were the high administrators in the civil service.

FREEMEN

This was a class of men and women that grew as the slave population grew in numbers and in power. At first they were merely those slaves set free by humane or kindly masters. Often this freedom was given as payment for loyalty, or in the case of a female slave, because the owner had children by her and wanted to marry her and legitimize their children. At first they could only exercise the vote inside the city but in 312 BCE they were given the same rights as other citizens. As these freemen were often working successfully in business in the city it gave them considerable power.

OPTIMATES

In the early days of the republic the affairs of state were determined by debate in the Senate. Inevitably it was a small number of conservative influential families who carried through the laws and controlled elections. This group was known as the Optimates. These traditionalist political power brokers came under threat from the more radical and younger members of their own class, the Populares.

PATRICIANS

The patricians were a small group of wealthy families with political influence and an enhanced social position. They dominated the Senate and initially ensured that the plebeians were kept out. They maintained their power by gathering around them individuals who relied on their influence to protect and advance them. The patricians grew in influence and power as their wealth increased, mostly through cattle rearing. They held all the priestly offices, which meant that they controlled the magistracy and the consulship as they controlled the reading of the auspices that gave advice from the gods. Eventually the distinction between the patrician and plebeian (see below) classes became blurred.

PLEBEIANS

These were not high-ranking men and were kept out of public office by the patricians (see above). This exclusion ceased when the plebeians demanded and achieved their own collegium in which their tribunes became extraordinarily powerful. In 287 BCE, as a result of wielding the power of their numbers, they gained social and political rights that were equal to those of the patricians. They achieved power by wielding their undoubted strength in the streets with leaders who were not afraid to rabble rouse if the necessity arose.

PRAETOR

A Praetor was the head of the judicial business of Rome. As this business increased a second praetor was appointed whose main area of work was to guide disputes between foreigners and Roman citizens. He might well be specialized in a particular area of law. In the period of the Roman Empire they were replaced by praetorian prefects who were in effect ministers in control of the emperor's council. A man had to be 40 before he could become a praetor.

QUAESTOR

The appointment as quaestor was the beginning of a Roman official's career. Initially it had been an office dating from the kingdom to deal with matters of law. In the period of the republic a quaestor was a magistrate who specialized in financial matters and answered only to the consuls. To be appointed as quaestor a man had to be 28 years old. It was an important rite of passage for any ambitious Roman man.

SENATE

Originally the members of the Senate were exclusively patricians (see above). During the period of the Roman Republic and until the plebeians gained the franchise they were the real focus of power. When Augustus became emperor the Senate was allowed to feel that it had parallel power with the Emperor. But in fact he kept the real power to himself while allowing the Senate a token of its past strength. The power of the Senate was eroded by successive emperors.

While many of its members were against democracy, which was initially advocated by men such as Brutus and Cicero, the Senate was also opposed to the return of the monarchy. Members of the Senate were rich, well placed and influential and while domestic political power eventually swung to the equestrian class (see above) the Senate did produce the men capable of realizing Rome's aspirations to expansion.

TRIBUNE

These were magistrates with many duties both political and military. They were appointed by the *Comitia Tributa*, which was an assembly elected by the plebeians. Only those who had been adopted or born plebeians could become tribunes of the people. Tribunes had the power of veto against magistrates. They could arrest and fine people and they organized and controlled public meetings. The civil power of the tribunes was wide ranging and their military power lay with levying troops for the Roman army.

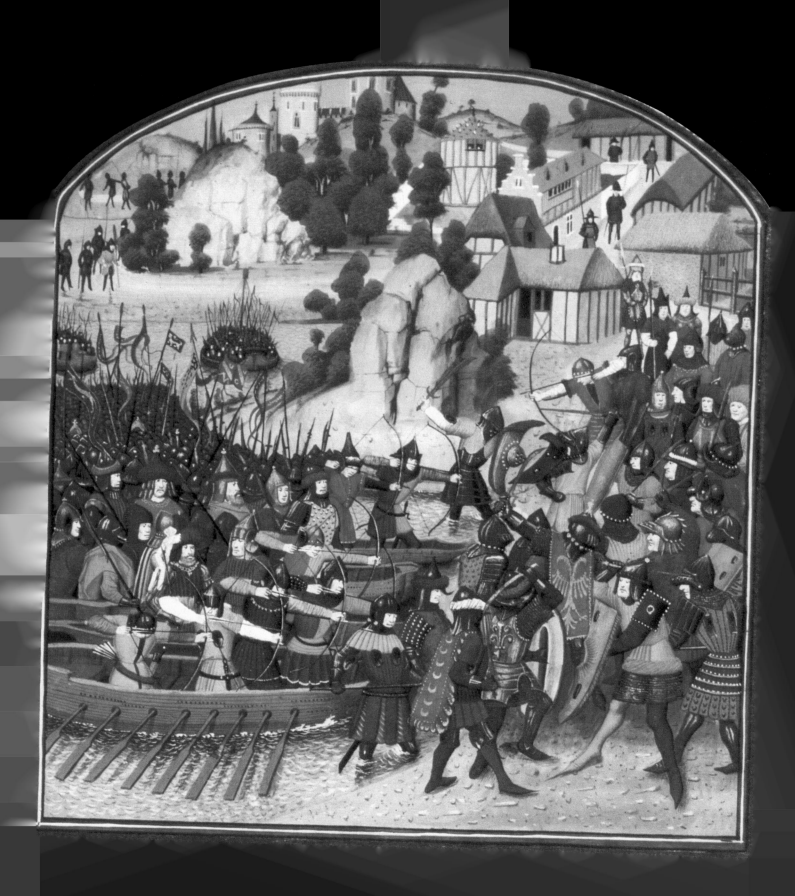

Caesar and the Conquest of Gaul

CHAPTER III

CAIUS JULIUS CAESAR was born into a patrician family in Rome on July 13, 100 BCE. A quick-witted and intelligent boy, he was brought up with many advantages. Yet his family was not rich by the fabulously wealthy standards of many at that time. Lack of money could prove to be a handicap to any ambitions that the young Caesar might have for a life at the forefront of Roman society.

Caesar proudly claimed to be descended from Venus (Aphrodite) and Anchises, father of Aeneas and ancestor of Romulus, the founder of Rome. His mother, Aurelia, was from a powerful family, although they had plebeian roots. The Caesars lived in modest circumstances in an unremarkable area of the city where Julius received the usual schooling for a boy of his background. It seems he had a facility with languages. The usual military training of a patrician youth would have been part of his normal routine—mastery of sword and spear were expected and he appears to have been a particularly good horseman.

At around the age of 14 Caesar was engaged to marry Cossutia who was, according to the Greek writer Plutarch, from a family of the equestrian caste. Despite being lower on the social scale, her family was rich, which had to be a consideration for Caesar's parents when they chose her as a wife for their son. A year later, Caesar's father died. ❦

OPPOSITE *Julius Caesar lands on the English coast in 55 BCE. From an illuminated manuscript c. 1454–1460.*

However impeccable his aristocratic background and however much Julius proved to have a fine and able intelligence, lack of money was a constant problem. Nevertheless, the family did have some influential connections. Caesar's favorite aunt, Julia, had married Gaius Marius in 113 BCE (see panel). Marius was an influential politician, who did not tolerate fools and vigorously opposed the arrogance of the patricians in the Senate.

He was a fine if impetuous general and was involved in reforming the Roman army. He was also a leading democrat, intent on confronting the conservative wing of the Senate. He had clawed his way to political prominence despite being born outside Rome to a family that did not even have the right to vote.

Because of his contentious nature, the influence Gaius Marius could wield for Caesar was something of a double-edged sword. The ambitious young man had to make some moves for himself. Caesar decided to abandon Cossutia and instead married Cornelia, the daughter of Lucius Cornelius Cinna (130–84 BCE), a politician of note who had been elected consul in 87 BCE. The young Caesar may have decided this union was an astute move into the political arena.

The conflict between Marius and Sulla (see page 34) provided the backdrop and the political experience that helped young Caesar's gradual rise to power. Sulla became a consul in 88 BCE and was subsequently sent by the Senate to confront King Mithridates of Persia. Taking advantage of his absence, Marius pushed through reforms of the Senate, cutting back its power and influence.

When Sulla learned about this, he returned at the head of his army, crushed Marius and his supporters and declared himself sole ruler—dictator—of Rome. It was the first time that a Roman general had ever used his military command against the city. Sulla restored the privileges of the Senate, reformed and weakened the public institutions, and had a number of his opponents killed. He was a ruthless political operator and to stand in his way was to invite danger.

Caesar was a man on the rise and Sulla considered him a potential enemy. Through his family ties to Marius, who died in 86 BCE, he was connected to the Democrat Party, and through his marriage he was connected to Cinna, an outspoken enemy of Sulla.

Despite his youth, Caesar was proving to be a good public orator. His speeches were greeted with delight by those who were opposed to the conservative patrician power brokers. In the hotbed of political infighting, Sulla began a campaign to destroy the ambitious young man through intimidation and threat. It was a true baptism of fire.

Sulla stripped Caesar of his inheritance and ordered him to divorce Cornelia, but the young man refused and was forced into hiding. Sulla used

OPPOSITE *A marble bust of the young Gaius Julius Caesar made during the first century BCE.*

GAIUS MARIUS

Gaius Marius was born in about 157 BCE to an equestrian family at Arpinum, which was also the home of the great orator Cicero. Marius was an ambitious and determined man and saw a way out of the poverty of peasant farming by joining the army. He was voted a tribune of the people in 119 BCE and served in Spain as praetor (law official), which gave him experience in government. He then served in Numidia (Northwest Africa) in campaigns against the region's king, Jugurtha. In 107 BCE Marius was elected to the position of consul, although he continued to command armies during the Teuton and Cimbri invasions of Italy.

Marius was an important figure in the fight against the power of the patricians, who controlled the Senate. They resisted him because of his low birth, but he still managed to implement reforms in the army. He believed these changes, which affected the system of enlistment, armaments and the organization of the legions, were essential if the Roman army was to avoid unnecessary defeats.

The changes made by Marius made the army a profession that was open to all free-born citizens, rather than just the aristocratic classes. A legion was now to be 6,000 men and was given its own eagle standard. The cohort was to consist of 600 men, each armed with a pilum. One drawback of his changes meant that each legion had to depend on a particular commander and because the appointment of generals was in the hands of the Senate, it opened the way for the appointment of men who were not always suitable for command.

RIGHT *A marble bust of Gaius Marius (157–86 BCE), a reforming politician and tribune of the people.*

his secret agents to try to find him, so Caesar had to move every night to avoid the assassination squads. It was only because of the intervention of his family and friends that he was not killed during Sulla's killings. Sulla pardoned him reluctantly and according to Suetonius said to the relatives: "Very well, take him but do not forget that the man you want me to spare will one day be the ruin of the party we have long defended. There are many Mariuses in this Caesar."

CAESAR AND THE PIRATES

Rhodes lay in an area of the Mediterranean that was dominated by pirates who specialized in kidnap, extortion and blackmail. The families of victims knew that if they didn't pay the ransom demanded the victim would never return. After his capture, Caesar was taken to their stronghold, where it seems that they took him for a wealthy Roman. They had no idea that they had captured one of the most distinguished and brave soldiers in the Roman army who had very little money. He was, after all, a very young man. When the pirate leader told him that he had asked as much as 20 talents in ransom Caesar appeared to be offended—"Ask 50 at least," he demanded.

The pirates sent Caesar's traveling companions back to Rome with the ransom demand. They were told they had only 40 days to collect the money or their friend would die. It appears that the pirate chief and Caesar got on well. They joked, played games, talked and ate together like good friends. Julius told his captor that if he regained his freedom he would come back and take not only the ransom but the lives of the entire pirate gang too. The pirate laughed at the very idea.

As the deadline for the ransom loomed, even the pirate chief seemed to be concerned that the money should arrive and he would be able to let his victim go free with honor. After 38 days, the money was paid. Caesar was free. He reminded his captors of his promise, telling them that they would have done better to kill him, as he was going to return and kill them. They laughed in his face, they didn't believe that Caesar would dare to return. They had completely misread this man as other, better men did in the future.

The moment he reached safety, Caesar organized a fleet. He led it back to the pirates' base and the gang was defeated, as Caesar had promised. He was asked what was to be done with the men among whom he had lived for nearly two months. They may have hoped for freedom, for they had not harmed him and they had let him go free. These were men he admired for their skills and their courage, and they hoped he might show them mercy.

But Caesar reminded them that he too kept his word. He had scaffolds constructed and ordered that they all be crucified. To make their deaths a little easier, and because he respected them as warriors, he ordered that their throats be cut before they were nailed to the crosses. Julius Caesar had proved that he was already a ruthless and a merciless opponent. He was still just 24 years old.

Caesar Joins the Army

Julius Caesar had already wisely decided that Rome might become too dangerous for him and he left the city. He was deeply in debt and needed to escape his creditors. Joining the army might give him a chance to win some prize money and so settle his debts.

He served under Marcus Themus in Asia and then under the command of Lucius Lucullus, during which time he was awarded a crown of oak leaves for his bravery in battle and for saving a fellow soldier's life. Caesar was coming to the notice of the right people and above all was gaining a reputation among his men for concern for the safety of the soldiers he commanded. It was a reputation he carried with him to later commands and to more important battles.

In 79 BCE Sulla retired to his home outside Rome and died a year later. Caesar was serving in Cilicia under Servilius when he heard the news and he returned to Rome in 78 BCE. With Sulla dead, the most dangerous threat to his political future had been removed. Caesar was determined that the reforms instigated by the dictator should be repealed and that power should be taken back from the magistrates and the Senate and given to the tribunes of the people. Caesar was offered advancement by the consul Marcus Aemilius Lepidus, who headed the political revolt after Sulla's retirement. He wisely turned down the offer, as he was not confident that Lepidus had the mettle for the political battles ahead. He was right. The revolt was put down.

In 76 BCE Caesar decided to go to Greece to study at the training school for rhetoric under the best living practitioner, Apollonius Molo. On his way to the eastern Mediterranean he was captured by pirates off the island of Pharmacussa, near Rhodes (see panel).

The Political Career Begins

In 68 BCE Cornelia died while giving birth to a stillborn son (the couple already had a daughter named Julia). Caesar was broken-hearted. In the same year his Aunt Julia also died. He used the funerals to make his first openly political move, giving orations in honor of the two women while ensuring that the funeral mask of Marius was paraded as a direct signal of his opposition to Sulla's changes in the constitution. He also

remarried, taking Sulla's granddaughter, Pompeia, as his bride.

The same year Caesar was elected to the position of quaestor in southern Spain and Portugal. While there he attacked independent tribes and made enough money to settle his debts. He returned to Rome and was elected as aedile (magistrate) in 65 BCE. Caesar was climbing the political ladder at the same time as ensuring his connections with people of influence. The great general Pompey (Magnus Pompeius) wanted to continue the war in the east, a plan that was supported by Caesar, who gained himself a powerful ally in doing so. At about the same time he made a friend of Marcus Licinius Crassus (c. 115–153 BCE), a fabulously wealthy Roman, who provided much financial support for this politician on the rise.

Caesar needed to ensure that he had a source of funds if he was to make his next ambitious move. The populace were always volatile, which made them difficult to keep calm. His position as aedile meant that he had the responsibility for the daily running of the growing city and also had to organize and fund the Roman games. Caesar could not afford to get things wrong. The moment of maximum risk and of maximum potential gain had arrived and Caesar made a spectacular decision. He risked all on creating the most magnificent games he could not afford. It was a triumph. Caesar owed hundreds of gold talents at the end of it, although Crassus paid off the debt.

In his book *The Twelve Caesars* Suetonius describes Caesar as a man given to plots and plotting. In 63 BCE a conspiracy to overthrow the magistrates and seize the consulship was revealed by the senior consul, Marcus Tullius Cicero. The leader of the conspiracy was said to be Lucius Catalina (Cataline) of the patrician party. Cicero's revelation was enough for five important Roman

RIGHT *Cicero (106–43 BCE): orator, politician and writer. A marble portrait bust of Caesar's enemy.*

men to be sentenced to death. Caesar was vehemently opposed to this judicial murder but he had against him a consistent and long-time personal enemy, Marcus Porcius Cato, the leader of the patrician Optimate party.

The two men met in public and debated their arguments, Caesar lost the discussion and the five men were promptly executed. Caesar was left with bad blood between himself and Cato and Cicero.

Caesar very much wanted a command in Egypt, where the pharaoh Ptolemy XIII had been deposed. As Ptolemy was a client of Rome, Caesar felt it was right that his rule be reestablished. It would be an opportunity to build up his funds as Ptolemy was offering a large inducement to whoever would help him. The ruling patricians vetoed his request. But Caesar had his revenge. He

used his position as aedile to arrange an exhibition of all the public monuments commemorating the victories of Marius, who stood for everything the patricians despised. He also prosecuted the men who had made money by bringing in Roman citizens outlawed during Sulla's massacres.

The First Triumvirate

In 62 BCE Pompey returned to Rome from his wars in the east, where he had achieved great triumphs. He had defeated Mithridates in Persia, added Syria and Judaea to the list of Roman territories and made vast amounts of money. There was a natural fear that he would do as Sulla had done and arrive with his army and become dictator. He disbanded his troops to whom he had promised grants of land from the Senate as reward for their service.

Cato led the Senate in refusing to give Pompey any of the things he had promised his soldiers. The city was in turmoil as Crassus prepared his forces in case Pompey made a move on the city. Crassus did not trust Pompey as they had their differences when they had served as consuls.

However, in 60 BCE Caesar brokered a peace between the two men and the trio formed a secret alliance, swearing to oppose any legislation of which any of them disapproved. In 59 BCE Caesar was elected to the highest Roman office when he became consul, and that year he married his third wife, Calpurnia, having divorced Pompeia. Using a series of questionable tactics, the Triumvirate came to dominate the Senate. They made the position of Caesar's fellow consul impossible; they bribed a man to testify that members of the Senate had tried to make him assassinate Pompey and they forced another senator, Lucullus, to his knees to beg Caesar's pardon for opposing his policies. The Triumvirate was flexing its muscles.

This alliance between Pompey, Crassus and Caesar was cemented when Caesar's daughter Julia married Pompey. In order to do this, Caesar broke her previous engagement to a fellow Roman who had given him much support in the recent struggles against the Senate.

Caesar was now in a position to ensure that he got exactly what he wanted. He had risked all the money he had on political deals and bribery, and he needed to rebuild his funds. He wanted to be given a large province to control or an undefeated country to engage in battle. Initially, the Senate gave him Cisalpine Gaul to govern, but Caesar wanted more, so he was given Transalpine Gaul as well.

With his affairs in Rome in the hands of Pompey and Crassus, Caesar now looked to the rest of Gaul. Once he had conquered Gaul, he could return to Rome a wealthy man and implement the greatest and most ambitious of his plans. Caesar saw no limit to what he could achieve. The Gallic campaigns would make him wealthy enough to buy and blackmail, to extort and to cajole the Romans into doing what he wanted. If they refused he would have a loyal, tried and tested army under his control. Pompey would perhaps stand in his way, but Caesar had no fear of him. Sulla had shown him that the path to victory lay in creating loyal legions. To do that all he had to do was lead them to victory.

LEFT *Marcus Licinius Crassus (c. 115–153 BCE), a wealthy supporter of the ambitious young Caesar. One of the first Triumvirate with Pompey and Caesar.*

LICINIO CRASSO

THE GALLIC WARS

58 BCE	Caesar defeats the Helvetii
	Campaign against German invaders of Gaul
57 BCE	Campaign against Belgae
56 BCE	Campaign in Brittany against Veniti
	Campaign against Aquitani in SW France
	Campaign in northern Gaul
55 BCE	Invades Britain
54 BCE	Winter quarters on Rhine
53 BCE	Campaign on Rhine and then forced march into Holland to fight Menapii
	Caesar crosses Alps to winter in Italy
52 BCE	Rising in southern Gaul and Arverni (Auvergne)
	Defeat and capture of Vercingetorix
51–50 BCE	Consolidation of Roman conquest of Gaul

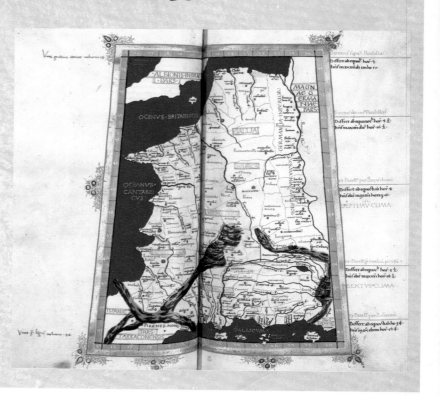

RIGHT *A map of Gaul and the southern coast of England from Ptolemy's* Cosmography.

The Gallic Wars, 58–51 BCE

Caesar spent seven years in the conquest of Gaul, an area that included all of modern France, Switzerland and northern Germany (see panel). Plutarch claims that 800 towns were destroyed and a million lives were lost on the side of the Gauls. The Senate might have had great misgivings about allowing this clever and ambitious man free reign in Gaul, but they may well also have hoped that at 40, he might fail, be disgraced and ruined.

There were those in the Senate already at work trying to separate Pompey from his fellows in the Triumvirate. Crassus was anxious to go to war in Syria and Pompey had misgivings about the way in which Caesar had consolidated his hold on the institutions of law and order in Rome. For the moment Pompey held his peace, but as Caesar later realized matters were not entirely under control in the city.

Cisalpine Gaul was the corridor along both banks of the River Po, which had been settled by Celtic tribes from Gaul. The Romans controlled a corridor along the Mediterranean that allowed them to move freely across the Rhone down into their Spanish colonies. As a result of pleas by some Gallic settlements, Caesar attacked the Helveti, 400,000 of whom had moved from their homes on the west of Switzerland to invade Gaul. Caesar harried them north along the Arar (the Saône) and totally defeated them at Bibracte (Autun). Then he dealt with the German tribes, 20,000 of which had moved into Gaul under their leader Ariovistus. Caesar demanded that Ariovistus remove his troops from Gaul. The German chief refused. Caesar had to work hard on the morale of his army to persuade them to confront the terrifying German warriors. Being the natural leader he was, Caesar's confidence spread to his men.

Caesar's troops occupied a fortress at Vesontio (Besançon) and drove the Germans back across the Rhine after destroying their army in the south of Alsace. One of the key aspects of his campaigns was the speed at which Caesar moved his troops. They thought nothing of a three-day

OPPOSITE *A triumphal arch at Carpentras showing Gallic prisoners-of-war in chains with their weapons beside them. First century CE.*

ABOVE *A crossing of the Rhine showing the hills and forests beyond the river and the German border.*

forced march before going straight into battle.

At the Rhine, Caesar gained the confidence of the Triboci nobles. He may have bribed them, but they agreed to act as border guards to keep their own countrymen behind the line of the river.

After a winter in camp among friendly tribes, the legions turned against the Belgae who had formed a confederacy. At the River Axona (Aisne) the confederacy fell apart and Caesar mopped up each tribe separately. It was an easy campaign, except when the Nervii surprised his legions as they made camp. Caesar had to pull the men together by stepping into the ranks himself and fighting alongside his legionaries. The Nervii were almost annihilated as a result.

Caesar imbued his commanders the confidence that they could take on any enemy in any place. In the north and west the Veniti were as at home on the sea as any Bretons. He sent a lieutenant to take them on. The lieutenant had ships built and raided the enemy fortresses along the coast until the Veniti surrendered. Meanwhile in the southwest the Aquitani were defeated by Publius Crassus, another of Caesar's young officers and the son of his wealthy ally. At the same time Caesar marched north against the tribes near the Channel coasts and wintered there.

There were attacks on three fronts and each resulted in victory for Caesar. It was a masterly campaign. He determined to invade Britain where, according to Suetonius, he believed a conquest "was most likely to enrich him and furnish suitable material for triumphs. They say he invaded Britain in the hope of getting pearls that he could weigh in his own hand. He was always a most enthusiastic collector of gems, carvings and pictures and also of slaves of exceptional figure and training. He paid so much for these slaves that he forbade the entry into his accounts."

However, the first attempt on Britain in 55 BCE gained little and the second very little more. Dio Cassius wrote in *Roman History*: "From Britain he had won nothing for himself or the state except the glory of having conducted an expedition against its inhabitants. Romans at home magnified his achievement to a remarkable degree."

Which was exactly what he wanted. Caesar needed the mob behind him and the best way to achieve that was to make sure they had historic victories to celebrate. *His* victories. As Plutarch noted in *Caesar* he had the courage to push the boundaries of the empire beyond the known world. In this he had achieved the sort of fame and adulation that he knew would serve him well when he returned to Rome.

He had achieved the two things he set out to do. He had subdued the Gauls taking vast amounts of loot as a result. He had continually sent news to Rome of his progress and of his gains and the citizens of the city were eager for him to return in triumph.

Most importantly for him he had forged a bond between himself and his soldiers that would serve him well in the future. Plutarch again sums up this achievement by retelling a story, which puts Caesar in a good light.

He was so much master of the good-will and willing service of his soldiers that ordinary men were changed under his command and displayed a courage past defeating. They would go into any danger where Caesar's glory was concerned ... In Britain, when some of the senior officers had got into a bog where they were assaulted by the enemy, a common soldier, whilst Caesar stood and looked on, threw himself in the middle of them, and bravely rescued the officers and beat off the barbarians.

In the end this brave soldier swam and waded out of the bog. In the clinging mud he lost his shield. Caesar and his officers saw his bravery and met him with delight. But the soldier, ashamed and in tears, threw himself down at Caesar's feet and begged his pardon for having let go his shield.

This love of honor and passion for distinction were

inspired in them by Caesar who by his unsparing distribution of money and honors, showed them that he did not heap up wealth from the wars for gratifying his private pleasures. That he looked upon all he gave to deserving soldiers as so much increase to his own riches. . . . Added to this also, there was no danger to which Caesar did not willingly expose himself, no labor from which he pleaded an exemption.

Plutarch's story may or may not be true, but is no doubt how the legions saw their leader under whose command they gained loot, fame, honor and victory. Caesar continued to consolidate his victories over the various tribes in Gaul. Some agreed to give him hostages, others conceded victory and gave him gold, others promised to join him. Caesar even created a legion from Gauls who wanted to fight under his command. But there were those who still refused to bend the knee and others who were ready for revolt if a suitably charismatic leader appeared.

In 52 BCE the Arverni from southern Gaul, found such a leader in a warrior called Vercingetorix. He had decided that confronting the Roman army head-on was a foolish tactic and began to use a scorched-earth policy to deny the Roman legions food or shelter wherever they moved. Caesar and his legions harried him through the Loire valley, crossed the Cevennes in the dead of winter and took Bourges, which the inhabitants had refused to burn as Vercingetorix had demanded. Former allies of Rome joined Vercingetorix in a general revolt. It was essential for Caesar to destroy this warrior chief. He turned south and Vercingetorix attacked the Romans and was forced to retreat to an utterly impregnable fortress near Dijon called Alesia.

Here Caesar demonstrated his formidable military talents and here the battle for Gaul was won and lost. After it was over Caesar took reprisals of a savage nature on those tribes who had betrayed him, took hostages from all the tribes and also took tribute in slaves and jewels, in corn and horses, in gold and land. Gaul would not revolt or threaten Rome in his lifetime. Caesar turned and crossed the Alps into Cisalpine Gaul and headed towards the River Rubicon, the boundary that stood between him and Rome.

In Rome they saw Caesar's ambition and were afraid. Pompey and the Senate forbade Caesar to advance into Italy from Gaul. Caesar knew that

the Senate was not going to make him an officer of state for a further term. He also knew that if he abandoned his army to return to Rome he would not survive. Even Pompey had turned against him since his wife Julia, Caesar's daughter, had died. Camped on the other side of the River Rubicon with the XIII Legion, Caesar had to make up his mind.

BELOW *Vercingetorix, the leader of the Gauls who fought against Caesar from 52 BCE until his own surrender at Alesia seven years later.*

QVANTA STRA
GE VIRVM SVBLI
MIS ALEXIA CESSIT
CÆSAREIS AQVI
LIS. PICTA TABEL
LA NOTAT

THE BATTLE OF ALESIA

THE FINAL BATTLE between Vercingetorix and Caesar and his legions is an epic example of the skill and leadership of the Romans and the courage of those they had to defeat to secure their territories. Caesar was constantly aware of the activities of the leader of the Arverni and in 53–52 BCE Vercingetorix led a massive revolt of Gallic tribes against the Romans.

Vercingetorix persuaded these tribes to unite in an alliance against Rome. His warriors used the tactic of attacking and then retreating into prepared fortifications. Vercingetorix also razed the ground behind him if he was forced to retreat. He destroyed all villages and farms and any sources of supplies and food for the enemy. This was a serious threat to the Roman army, which was accustomed to living off the land.

According to *Gallic Wars*, which he wrote after the events, Caesar called his men together and told them that their objective was to destroy these warriors, to capture their baggage trains and scatter their cavalry. He wrote that when he described his vision of how this campaign would be fought, his cavalry shouted out: "we shall swear by the most sacred oath that any one of us who has not ridden through the enemy's army twice shall be cast out, shall have no access to his children, his parents or his wife…"

The Romans confronted the Gauls, routed them and took some of their leaders, but they failed to capture or kill Vercingetorix. He, having lost his cavalry, was now forced to fight from a fixed point. He fortified the town of Alesia, which was already well protected. The settlement stood on a hill, protected on two sides by rivers and surrounded by a wall against which the Gauls piled stone walls six feet high.

The Romans protected their positions below the city with a trench that was 11 miles (18 km) long. They built towers along a wall behind the trench and set guards. The scene is described in *Gallic Wars*.

The enemy sent out the remains of their cavalry to charge Caesar's men. Caesar sent the German auxiliaries to support his men and the enemy fled back to the narrow city gate. The German cavalry slaughtered them in their hundreds as they tried to cram into the gates. Some of the enemy even left their horses and tried to climb the walls to safety.

Caesar ordered the legions he had drawn up in front of the ramparts to advance a little.

This caused the Gauls to panic. Vercingetorix ordered the gates to be closed and the slaughter went on. Vercingetorix, that night, decided that the cavalry he had left were of little use and, to save them and their horses, he smuggled them out of the town at nine in the dark of night. They escaped through the last gap in the Roman siege line.

Vercingetorix ordered all the corn in the camp to be brought to him under pain of death and doled out a ration man to man. He did the same with the cattle, which were within his camp. So prepared, he waited for the reinforcements he had sent for.

OPPOSITE *The siege of Alesia showing the fortifications. Oil on wood by Feselen (d. 1538).*

BELOW *A detailed model of Caesar's lines of defense at the siege of Alesia. Ditches, stakes and hidden ditches. French, nineteenth century.*

RIGHT *A Gaulish bronze helmet with cheek guards from the battlefield of Alesia. First century BCE.*

sharpened and fire-hardened stakes projecting a few inches above the ground. These were secured with tamped clay and then the whole covered with brushwood and twigs to hide them. Eight rows of these were dug. The soldiers called this "the lily" because it looked like the flower. In front of these, stakes a foot long with iron hooks were entirely sunk into the ground. These all faced the encircled enemy in the city.

Now he turned and made exactly the same fortification behind him. He had created a secure place that could be defended by a few soldiers if his men were called away for any reason. Vercingetorix was walled inside his defenses.

Caesar now ordered every man to provide himself with forage and corn for 30 days. He heard from spies that debates were held inside the enemy camp. Some wanted to confront the enemy as a matter of honor. Others counselled caution.

The first argument won. Bringing out ladders and hurdles to cross the ditches the Arverni advanced from their fortress to the Roman army waiting for them.

The Gauls grew overconfident when they killed some Romans. Caesar ordered the German cavalry to show themselves and the Gauls panicked. The Romans attacked ruthlessly as the German cavalry surrounded the Gallic archers and slaughtered them where they stood. The Gauls retreated. The Arverni returned to the attack at midnight and were thrown back from the Roman fortifications by slings, arrows and stones and because of the stakes that defended the ramparts. The Roman field commanders sent in reinforcements and, in the dark, the Gauls impaled themselves on the stakes and "lilies" in front of the ditches.

Later Vercingetorix attacked yet again with scaling ladders, hooks, and movable siege towers and for a time it seemed as if victory would be his. But Caesar was watching it all from a hilltop and sent fresh men to reinforce the most threatened places.

The Gauls cannot penetrate the Roman front line. The Romans advanced into their enemy in the almost impregnable formation known as the "testudo." The Gauls give way. But now the Romans in the front line are exhausted.

Caesar sends Labienus with six cohorts to relieve

Caesar heard this from deserters and resolved to take the war to the enemy. First he dug a line of trenches 20 feet (6 meters) deep with steep sides. He then made the rest of his fortification 400 feet (120 meters) back from the ditch out of range of enemy javelins or arrows.

He dug two trenches 15 feet (4.5 meters) wide and 15 ft (4.5 meters) deep. The innermost being on low and level ground he filled with water drawn from the river. Behind it he raised a rampart and wall 12 feet (3.6 meters) high with battlements and parapets and pointed stakes projecting from it to stop the enemy climbing the wall. He surrounded the entire work with turrets 80 feet (25 meters) from each other.

Caesar commandeered supplies of corn and timber from the nearby farms. He designed ways to make his fortifications defensible by a small number of men. More trenches were dug with sharp stakes in the bottom interlaced with other stakes to impale any charging attackers.

In front of them shallower trenches had more

these men. Caesar shows himself to them... "The thin faced, purple clad warrior."

Still the Gauls come on and with huge numbers of missiles and, fighting from the siege towers they have brought with them, they fill in the ditches with clay and hurdles, and tear down the ramparts with hooks.

The Romans stand steady as ordered. They are fighting hand to hand now using their swords and knives and as they do so Caesar sends in more cavalry to the rear of the Gauls. They turn to run and are trapped between the foot soldiers and the cavalry and a great slaughter ensues.

It was a timely tactical move. Now comes perhaps the noblest moment recorded by Caesar and it does not concern him but his enemy, Vercingetorix.

As his men fled from the slaughter Vercingetorix called together his council and spoke to them,

"I undertook this war, not for myself but for the cause of our freedom. Since we have not had victory on our side I offer myself to you. You must use me as you feel is best. Either offer me alive to the Romans so that I may atone to them for what we have done under my leadership. Or kill me and give them my body...Either way you may not suffer for what we have tried to do together."

Seven years after Vercingetorix surrendered at Alesia, Caesar was granted a Triumph by the Senate. He rode through the streets of Rome and in the procession behind him followed the booty from his campaigns, the battle standards his men had won, the prisoners and slaves they

BELOW *The savagery of warfare during Caesar's Gallic Campaign at Alesia. Stone relief carving.*

had captured, the horses, chariots, and the riches he had gained were displayed as the legions marched with him. Among this booty was the greatest commander the Gauls had ever had.

Vercingetorix was still a young man. He was dressed in his armor on that day. His helmet was placed on his head but his hands and ankles were chained. And when Caesar had soaked up the roars of adulation from the crowd the Gaul's great chieftain was taken to the prison that had been his home for seven years and was duly strangled. Mercy to a brave enemy was not in Caesar's character.

ABOVE *Vercingetorix, an honorable man, surrenders himself to Julius Caesar to stop the slaughter of the Gauls in Alesia.*

Effudit dignas adytis è pectore voces.
" Quid quæri, Labiene, jubes? &c. ——
" An noceat vis ulla bono? fortunáque perdat
" Oppositâ virtute minas.'Laudandáque velle
" Sit satis, &nunquam succesfu crescat honestum.

M. ANNÆI LUCANI
PHARSALIA:
SIVE
DE BELLO CIVILI
INTER
Cæsarem & Pompeium
LIBRI DECEM.

LONDINI:
Ex Officinâ JACOBI TONSON,
& JOHANNIS WATTS.
MDCCXIX.
CVM PRIVILEGIO.

Civil War

CHAPTER IV

Whoever takes his way into a tyrant's court
Becomes his slave, although he went there a free man
Sophocles, Greek dramatist

WHILE CAESAR had been conquering Gaul, Rome had not been quiet. As the empire's borders had spread, the city itself had become a hotbed of social and political intrigue and of ill-disguised anger in the streets. The struggle between the various political interests caused great tension. Landowners wanted no change in their tenure to help the citizens without land; the Optimates (patricians) wished to retain control of the military to ensure their continued power; slave owners were at war with rebel slaves; and the privileged Roman citizens did not wish their advantages to be extended to other inhabitants of the empire.

The mob pursued their interests using violence, the patricians procured favors with bribes of money, food or the promise of advancement. The skillful way in which small concessions were granted meant that a full-blown revolution did not break out. §

OPPOSITE *The frontispiece of* Pharsalia, *an account of the civil war between Caesar and Pompey, written by Lucan (39–65 CE). An eighteenth-century engraving.*

The pressure on the Optimates came from young patricians who were often tribunes of the people working for their own interests. They wanted to weaken the Senate and tried to push through laws while ignoring the patrician interests. The patrician conservatives were also opposed by the commercial interests of the equestrians, who had business and trading links across Rome's colonies. This last group contained many military commanders.

The power of the First Triumvirate lay in the combination of Pompey, a relatively popular soldier and politician; Crassus, who understood business; and Caesar whose interests, even from distant Gaul, were served initially by a tribune

BELOW *A Roman bronze sesterce showing the Roman general Julius Caesar. His name is inscribed on the coin.*

named Publius Clodius. Clodius has been referred to as "the perfect master of disorder." As the tool of Caesar he was a leader of the mob. In 58 BCE, in a quest for popular support, Clodius demanded that corn distribution to the poor should be free. More dangerously, Clodius also made moves to rid the city of Cato and Cicero, the twin dangers to the First Triumvirate.

In a thinly disguised banishment, the Senate sent Cato to annex Cyprus. Cicero, who had condemned the Cataline conspirators to death, was confronted with a charge that he had violated a law that stated that no one could be executed without the vote of the people. Knowing that he was in danger, Cicero left Rome for Greece without disputing the charge. His house was burned by a violent mob organized by Clodius.

The Senate was appalled by these actions and called on all voters to come into the city to vote against this tribune's activities. The vote was eventually passed in 56 BCE, but Clodius was still a danger to ultraconservative patricians although he backed off when Pompey asked Cicero to return to Rome. When he came back to the city in 57 BCE Cicero was careful not to attack the First Triumvirate or its power bases.

However, there was a growing feeling that Caesar, Crassus and Pompey were no longer close.

With the Triumvirate apparently crumbling, Caesar left his army in Gaul and came to meet Pompey and Crassus at Lucca in northern Italy in an attempt to renew their alliance. Between them they carved up the power. Pompey and Crassus were to rule as consuls in 55 BCE and were to govern the provinces of Spain and Syria for five years, while Caesar was allowed to keep his Gallic command for the same period.

However, by 54 BCE Rome was descending into near anarchy. Titus Annius Milo, a rabble-rouser for the Optimate faction of the Senate confronted those who supported Caesar's ally Clodius. In 52 BCE both Milo and Clodius stood for the position of consul. Before the elections were held street brawls broke out between the rival factions. Milo's supporters trapped Clodius on the Appian Way and murdered him. Fury broke out in Rome for the murdered man had been a tribune of the people. Clodius's body was brought into the city and cremated in the Senate, which was burned to the ground at the same time.

Pompey took over as sole consul and attempted to restore order in Rome. When Milo stood trial for murder, Pompey ensured that he was found not guilty by packing the court with soldiers loyal to him. Pompey then made an agreement with the Senate that would end the Triumvirate. His family ties to Caesar were loosened with the death of his wife, Julia. Pompey, while not an adept politician, saw which way the wind was blowing and switched his support to patrician interests. When Crassus died in 53 BCE in a disastrous campaign against the Parthians at Carrhae the power of the First Triumvirate was at an end (see panel, page 66).

The Road to Civil War

In 50 BCE the struggle began between Caesar and the ultraconservative patrician families in the Senate. The patricians, as ever, wanted no changes that might erode their power. Caesar, with his rhetorical gifts, military skills and a huge number of supporters, was an obvious threat to their position. Although still in Gaul, Caesar was well aware of the dangers he faced in Rome. He bought the services of one Scribonius Curio, a young patrician tribune who was deeply in debt as a result of his debauchery. Curio, a very clever man, posed as an independent politician. He proposed to the Senate that both Caesar and Pompey should be obliged to give up their commands. Pompey refused to abandon his interests in Spain, as Curio knew he would. This allowed Caesar to refuse to give up his military command.

Pompey forbade Caesar to stand as consul in 49 BCE without giving up his military command and also refused to let him stand in absentia. He demanded that Caesar return to Rome, leaving his armies in place in Gaul. Caesar knew that if he returned to the city alone the Senate would charge him with irregularities during his command in Gaul. Pompey had clearly abandoned his old friend and father-in-law. Then a consul named Marcellus put forward a motion that Caesar should be declared a public enemy unless he agreed to surrender. When it was suggested that Caesar give up his command, Mark Antony (Marcus Antonius) and Quintus Longius Cassius supported their old friend and vetoed this motion. The Senate overthrew the veto. In doing this they had violated the sacred constitution and Caesar now had a semblance of legality on his side.

ABOVE *A silver sistophorus showing Mark Antony, c. 40 BCE. It was made at Ephesus to celebrate the temporary pact between Mark Antony and Octavian.*

ABOVE Caesar Crosses the Rubicon *painted on vellum by Jean Fouquet in the fifteenth century.*

Antony and Cassius fled Rome and joined Caesar. In open defiance of the Senate, Caesar and his army crossed the Rubicon and headed for Rome.

War Breaks Out

Rome became a city in turmoil with the news that Caesar had crossed the frontier with his soldiers. Caesar's force was small—he had only one legion available—and his men were lightly protected. But he knew he had support and that the army he had left behind in Gaul would join him if necessary. He had used some of the fortune he had amassed during the Gallic War to bribe men of ability and influence in Rome. Caesar was certain that he could remove Pompey, overcome the objections of the old patrician politicians and take sole power in the city.

Caesar split his forces. He advanced down the east coast of Italy while Antony occupied the western approach to Rome. Panic ensued. The Senate left Rome in the hands of the magistrates. Pompey, too slow to act, was driven south and sailed from Brundisium on March 17.

Caesar moved into Rome, where, much to their surprise, he treated his opponents mercifully. His first duty was to ensure stability in the city and to that end he arranged that Rome was fed. His lieutenants took control of Sicily and Sardinia, two islands that acted as granaries for Rome. He then turned to Spain, where he had to deal with Pompey's army. In a rapid and triumphant campaign he achieved this. Soldiers deserted to his side in vast numbers.

Throughout the year Caesar tried to pin Pompey down to fight. However, Pompey refused a pitched battle because he did not think his troops could defeat Caesar's smaller but more experienced army. Pompey moved the remnants of his force to Thessaly with the aim of extending Caesar's supply lines. Pompey had a problem with his aristocratic and precipitate lieutenants who were anxious to get back to Rome and to divide the spoils when Caesar was defeated. They were certain that he was about to be crushed. While Pompey wanted to keep Caesar at arm's length he knew he could not retain the support of these lieutenants if they did not have the opportunity to take on Caesar's army. Pompey brought the arguments to an end by confronting Caesar on the plain of Pharsalus (see panel).

His army scattered, Pompey fled to Egypt to restore his shattered hopes. Caesar followed him there, where he discovered that Pompey had become a player in the war between King Ptolemy and his wife and sister Cleopatra, who were involved in a struggle for the throne of Egypt. Yet again, Pompey showed how inept he was as a politician. He offered to throw in his lot with Ptolemy and was murdered on an Egyptian beach (see panel, page 60).

BATTLE OF PHARSALUS

ABOVE *A painting by Cassone on wood depicting the Battle of Pharsalus in which Pompey was defeated by Caesar.*

Caesar marched at great speed from his campaigns in Spain, crossed the Adriatic and found the legions under the command of Pompey, his former son-in-law and friend, at Pharsalus in Thessaly in August 48 BCE.

Caesar's small army was outnumbered by Pompey's force whose infantry were more than double in number and whose squadrons of cavalry were seven times larger. Pompey decided he could turn Caesar's right wing and then fall onto its rear. Caesar had guessed this would be Pompey's plan and so he had strengthened his cavalry force by placing among it some of his best infantry men.

This mixture of infantry and cavalry was a tactic he had confronted in his battles in Gaul. It is a measure of Caesar's skill as a general that he was willing to use alien tactics if he saw merit in them. Caesar kept six cohorts in reserve. Pompey's cavalry charged into the right of Caesar's position and found themselves balked by the infantry on that flank. Pompey's cavalry were not prepared and turned and raced in panic from the field. The panic spread and Pompey was left without an army. He too, fled.

Caesar had foreign prisoners put to death but Roman citizens were pardoned. Two of those he pardoned were Marcus Brutus and Gaius Longinus Cassius who four years later plotted against Caesar and assassinated him.

THE DEATH OF POMPEY

ABOVE *An idealized image of a funeral procession made in stone. At this funeral singers and mourners and priests make a stark contrast to the lonely funeral of Pompey.*

Plutarch described Pompey's death as being ordered by Ptolemy on the advice of a eunuch, a teacher of rhetoric and an Egyptian who were afraid that the Roman general might be coming to save Cleopatra.

It was some distance from the trireme to the land and Pompey, seeing that none of the company addressed a single friendly word to him, turned his eyes towards Septimus and said, "Surely I am not mistaken, you and I have been comrades in arms together." Septimus barely nodded and gave no sign of friendly feeling. Pompey took out a small book in which he had written down the speech he would make to Ptolemy. He began reading it to himself. On the trireme they watched the small boat and Cornelia his wife was apprehensive when she saw the army of Ptolemy lining the shore.

At this moment the small craft reached the shore. A soldier took Pompey's hand as if to steady him and Septimus ran him through from behind. Then the others took their daggers and stabbed him. Pompey drew his toga over his face, said nothing, groaned a little and died in his sixtieth year.

They cut off his head and threw his naked body into the shallow sea and left it for all to see. Pompey's former slave, Philip, washed the body when they had all left the beach. He wrapped it in cloth and began to search the beach for material with which to burn it. All he could find were the broken planks of an old and decaying fishing boat. It was enough to build a pyre.

An old man who had served as a youngster with Pompey came and asked what Philip was doing and the freeman told him. The old man begged him then, "Please… don't keep this honor for yourself but let me help for I shan't regret a lifetime spent in foreign places if I find the happiness at last to touch with my hands and wrap and prepare the body of the greatest commander Rome has ever seen for burial."

So Pompey came to his end.

Caesar in Egypt

Caesar stayed in Egypt, and became involved in the nation's political affairs. His forces were nearly defeated in Alexandria, the city founded by his hero, Alexander the Great. However, he called in reinforcements and destroyed Ptolemy's army, restoring Cleopatra, who became his mistress, to the throne. Before he left Egypt, accompanied by the Egyptian queen, he had time to father a son, Caesarion, with Cleopatra.

Caesar Returns to Rome

On his return to Rome Caesar restored order. Some of his legions had been causing trouble so Caesar had them paraded in front of him and addressed them merely as "citizens" and not as "soldiers." In doing this he was signaling their dismissal from the army, which shocked them deeply. They begged him to readmit them and he eventually agreed. They had learned their lesson.

In the city he was equally decisive, as there was no one left who dared to oppose him openly. This was the start of what has been described as "the hidden face of the new monarchy." Caesar's tough, radical and fair actions pulled Rome out of chaos. He dealt with problems caused by unfair taxation and appointed magistrates to oversee tax collection. He ensured the poor were fed and that the city and its institutions were in harmony. He knew that to ensure a lasting balance through the empire he had to confront those senators who had supported Pompey. Some had gone to North Africa where they were regrouping. In 46 BCE Caesar followed with his legions and moved to destroy the resurrected republican army at Thapsus. His army slaughtered as many as 50,000 men in a ruthless and merciless act. Among Caesar's opponents was Cato, who committed suicide because he had no hope left that the Roman Republic would return.

Caesar returned to Rome in triumph, the victor over Gaul, Egypt, Syria and Numidia. However, danger threatened in Spain where the rump of the Pompeian army had escaped from Africa. This army was even willing to take slaves into its ranks in its desperation to provide a force powerful enough to win the battle they knew was inevitable.

Caesar advanced into Spain in 45 BCE and the

CAESAR AND CLEOPATRA

Cleopatra was born in 69 BCE. She inherited the throne of Egypt in 51 BCE, which she was to share with her ten-year-old brother, Ptolemy XIII. They were to reign as husband and wife. However, in 48 BCE Ptolemy and his advisers had her removed from power. There are many stories about the way she first met Caesar, who was to restore her to her throne. It was difficult and dangerous for her to meet him openly. Caesar was regarded as an enemy by Ptolemy's advisers and they did not want him to meet the powerful and intelligent Cleopatra.

Petrach claims that she came to him at the palace in Alexandria, hidden in a rug. Caesar tried to arrange for reconciliation between her and her brother but at the banquet to celebrate this, Caesar's barber heard that the Egyptian General Achillas and the eunuch Pothinus, who had killed Pompey, were also planning to kill him. Caesar had Pothinus killed and went to war against Achillas. In 47 BCE he defeated Achillas and Ptolemy who vanished in the battle.

In 30 BCE Cleopatra proved as beguiling as ever when Mark Antony led the Roman army to Egypt (see pages 75–76). They became lovers and planned to remove Octavian (Augustus) and rule the Roman Empire together. When Augustus invaded Egypt, she attempted to work her charm on him but failed and poisoned herself with a deadly snake.

RIGHT *A sculpted bust of the seductive Cleopatra VII.*

final throw of the dice for the Pompeian party ended in a savage and bloody struggle at Munda where no quarter was asked or given. It was a terrible battle in which no prisoners were taken.

Caesar's phase of civil war was finished, but the second phase was to come very soon and it would be crueler than the first. For now Caesar turned his attention to the governance of Rome.

LEFT *A detail of the* Triumph of Caesar *in which captured treasures and prisoners of war would be shown to the Roman people. Made by Mantegna (1413–1506).*

Caesar, Master of Rome, 48–44 BCE

CHAPTER V

BETWEEN 48–44 BCE Caesar's ambitious plans began to bear fruit. During his Gallic campaign he had achieved many victories and through astute management of his interests in the city he had kept men of influence on his side. He was not trusted by the traditional patrician elements in the Senate, but even they could not dispute his consummate skill in creating a myth about himself and his wars on the frontiers of the empire. Through victory after victory and conquest after conquest this man was beloved of his soldiers and had managed to keep senatorial interference in his campaigns to a minimum. Caesar offered the people of Rome a possibility of stability and peace.

Caesar began the period of the First Civil War as a proconsul. He remained under threat from the Senate for his alleged illegal activities in Gaul, although in reality it was because they feared his ambition. Caesar would confront anyone who stood against him. When he crossed the Rubicon he had been courting danger, but within five years he obtained far more personal power than any Roman leader before him. He was showered with honors; given titles, decorations and adulation; and regarded as a living god. He treated the Senate with disdain. What he was not given in the way of power he took.

But, how had this happened in such a short period of time?

OPPOSITE *A stone statue of Julius Caesar triumphantly addressing the people.*

While his feats in battlefields from Gaul to Egypt, Spain to Greece and Numidia to Germany were sensational, how had Caesar managed to grasp so much political power in the city? During the time he spent on the campaigns to destroy the last vestiges of Pompey's armies, Caesar had left Rome under the rule of his proxies. In a city that was becoming almost ungovernable this could have created more problems than it solved.

Lepidus (see panel) was master of the few troops in the city and Mark Antony was too weak to prevent disorder breaking out. It would take a wise, subtle man or a strong, ruthless one to bring the city back to heel. For a time Caesar played wise and subtle, appearing to abide by the old Republican rules and systems.

Caesar was powerful enough though to ride roughshod over the constitution and with Pompey defeated and Crassus dead, he could dictate his terms. Some in the Senate suspected that Caesar had huge ambitions, but he was now too well placed to be stopped. From 49 BCE, the Senate allowed him to be elected consul for five years in succession. He was given control of issues of war and peace, and had the ability to nominate all officers of state except the plebeian positions. In short he was in virtually complete control of Roman political activity.

In 46 BCE, Rome held a Triumph in honor of Caesar's victories. He marched into the city at the head of the chariots and carts laden with the spoils of his victories—his soldiers called out mockingly that he had made himself the king. Members of the Senate may not have liked this, but there was nothing they could do except heap more honors on Caesar. The same year he was elected dictator for life. A statue was placed in the Capitol and with it his "divinity" was recognized. He was given sole command of the Roman army for life.

Caesar delegated power to his own officials, bypassing the elected magistrates. With his savage victory over the last of Pompey's supporters at Munda, the Senate became almost servile to him. But was this supine display of submission actually a means of making Caesar unpopular with the people? The centralization of power into his hands signalled the end of the Republic. He was even offered the crown by Mark Antony, although he refused the offer, as he realized that the position of king was repugnant to most Romans. But the offer was noted by those in the Senate who were implacably opposed to the idea of a dictatorship or one-man rule. Caesar misjudged the political climate when it became clear that he no longer deferred to the Senate in any way. Soon voices were whispering that the only solution to the threat Caesar posed was the assassin's dagger.

Caesar's Reforms

Rome was going through a period of financial problems and moneylenders were squeezing the people dry. Romans were being charged outrageous sums of interest on debts and troublemakers used this rapacity of the wealthy moneylenders to create trouble. Caesar decided to act with vigor and legislated against the moneylenders who were imposing cruel debts on their victims. Interest rates were lowered and controlled by law.

Caesar forbade the hoarding of money and anyone with more than 15,000 denarii was likely to lose it if it was discovered. Caesar also

LEPIDUS

Marcus Aemilius Lepidus was born into a patrician family in 89 BCE. He was made praetor in 49 BCE and consul in 46 BCE. Lepidus was one of Caesar's most enthusiastic supporters and proposed his dictatorship. While Caesar fought Pompey's supporters in Spain, Lepidus held control in Rome. After Caesar's assassination, he supported Mark Antony in a joint bid for power. He joined the Second Triumvirate (see page 73) and after surviving Octavian's victory he was made governor of Africa. In 36 BCE he made a move to take power in Sicily, but Octavian stripped him of all his offices and sent him into exile where he died peacefully in 13 BCE.

RIGHT *A bust of Marcus Lepidus (89–13 BCE), one of Julius Caesar's supporters. He suggested Caesar be made dictator.*

ordered that creditors should be bound to take the property of debtors at its value before the Civil War. Later he lowered the rent of tenements by a quarter and required that money be invested in land.

In the past he had used the disorders in Rome to his advantage but now he cracked down hard on rioters and on the mob. Caesar was determined that law and order should return to the city. He cut down the numbers of people flooding into the city for free corn. Those who wished to take advantage of this now had to provide officers with proof of their poverty and the ration was cut so that the number of recipients was halved from 300,000 to 150,000. He made land available to his war veterans, settling them in existing communities so that they integrated with the people and did not prove a focus for discontent.

Caesar was determined to initiate great public building schemes. The Pontine Marshes close to the city were drained to reclaim what were once malarial areas and provide fertile land for farmers. Road systems were enlarged and improved, with the work being done not only by slaves but also by freemen.

The infrastructure of local government changed so that towns and municipalities became independent of Roman magistrates. These were popular decisions among the plebeian supporters and had far-reaching effects on finance and controls of labor and taxes beyond Rome.

There was more to citizenship than being able to claim to be Roman. Caesar wanted Italy and the citizens beyond to be equal and he was determined that the franchise should be extended to any country, city or area that was ready. He controlled the depredations of provincial governors by cutting short their period in power and he also ensured that all their powers came under central control. They were not going to be allowed to amass power or money and thus become a threat to the state as he had been.

The borders of the empire were to be pushed forward in order to occupy the army. Caesar knew the dangers of allowing soldiers to sit in barracks idly waiting for action. They could become eager listeners to anyone trying to make

trouble. By pushing out the frontiers he not only protected the provinces from the threat of barbarian invasions, but he also ensured that Rome was protected from the threat within.

These policies were guaranteed to make enemies of the people who already distrusted him. They were afraid that he would take over their power bases and marginalize them and it is true to say that they had good reason to believe it.

Here was a man who had clawed his way to his present position from a difficult beginning. He knew how ruthless men needed to be as a result of his early confrontation with Sulla and his secret police. He understood how the politics worked by watching the way his uncle Marius was ignored by the power brokers in the Senate. No one was going to stand in his way now. He had taken the power and he intended to use it. Who could stop him? He had neutralized the Senate and had no intention of returning Rome to its previous system. Caesar was not necessarily eager to be made king, as some claimed, but he was an

BELOW *A group of Senators together with the young son of a Senator. Marble relief from a sarcophagus found near Ostia, c. 270 CE.*

CRASSUS AT CARRHAE

Crassus had taken command of the Roman army in the province of Syria. From 54 to 53 BCE Crassus added to his immense wealth by plundering the nation. Then he crossed the Euphrates with a large army and began to make mistakes. The enemy, the Parthians, were a formidable force and any mistakes would be severely punished. Crassus was offered an alliance by the Armenian king who would have provided very mobile lightly armed troops to strengthen his forces. Crassus refused the offer. He then made a basic error by abandoning his defensive base line on the Euphrates and heading into the desert. He trusted his Arab guide who led him into an ambush at Carrhae. The Parthians, using light and fast cavalry surrounded the Romans.

Crassus formed the troops in close order rather than deploying them. It is a difficult problem to protect infantry in open ground against very mobile soldiers. Carrhae was a terrible defeat. The Romans were overrun and the aging Crassus went to a meeting with the enemy where he was murdered. It was a young quaestor who led the remnants of the troops back to what would become the permanent Roman frontier on the Euphrates.

OPPOSITE *Caesar leaves his distraught wife Calpurnia to walk to the Senate on the fateful Ides of March. This is a nineteenth-century painting by Abel de Pujol.*

BELOW *Marcus Junius Brutus, who may have been Julius Caesar's son, by Michelangelo. Marcus Junius Brutus acted against Caesar for the noblest motives.*

autocrat and determined that the Roman world would be ruled in his way. It was against this background that a group of conspirators was formed.

It was October 45 BCE and Caesar intended to leave on a campaign to avenge the death of Crassus who had died in battle in Asia (see panel).

The Ides of March

Caesar determined to take revenge for his old accomplice early in the next year and was already making preparations when fate began to catch up with him. There were omens of bad fortune—a comet passed through the sky, the sun faded and was faint at midday and an augur at the temple had warned him to "beware the Ides of March."

Men with messages called at Caesar's home on the morning before he set out for the Forum, but he did not have the time to read the warnings they brought. His powerful friend, Mark Antony, was detained outside the Senate House by Decimus Junius Albinius and so prevented from taking his usual place guarding Caesar. The conspirators' planning was meticulous, as it needed to be.

The plotters had diverse reasons for their actions. Some, such as Cicero, felt the loss of the power of the Senate, which, for them, was the repository of all that was good about Republican Rome. They knew the government was not perfect, that some of its members were corrupt, and that some indeed were too wedded to the old ways to be allowed to stand in the way of progress, but the Republican ideal was a bulwark against the monarchy that men like Cicero despised.

Others, like Decimus Junius Brutus, who had been such an avid supporter of Caesar, were part of the plot from which they felt they could personally gain. On the other hand there were men such as Marcus Junius Brutus, who may have been Caesar's son by his mistress Servilia, who mourned the loss of the Republican ideal.

These were the men who walked with Caesar as he came into the Senate House and went towards his chair. He was surrounded by men asking questions, calling and waving papers. Another of the conspirators, Tillius Cimber, was brother to a man Caesar had exiled and wanted him to be allowed to return to Rome. He was sure that if Caesar was killed his brother would be free to come home. Caesar brushed the request aside as others pressed around him more urgently.

Tillius pulled his toga down at the neck. This was the signal to attack. Cassius stabbed Caesar in the neck and wounded him. Then the others closed in on him like animals in a pack. Whichever way he turned he took the blows of the blades and saw the steel aimed at his face and eyes. Driven this way and that like a rat in a trap the blows slashed and stabbed down. Each of the conspirators had sworn to blood their knives in Caesar's body.

He fought them off as best he could, reeling from one to another until he saw Marcus Junius Brutus, whom he had loved and trusted. Brutus came in close with his bare blade and Caesar said "*Et tu Brute*" ("And you too Brutus"). Caesar then drew his toga over his head as he would when sacrificing at an altar and took Brutus's blade in his groin. In all he took 23 wounds and died as Senators turned and ran, leaving the conspirators reeking of the blood of Caesar.

The mangled body lay at the foot of the statue of Pompey. It was March 15, 44 BCE. Julius Caesar was dead and civil war would return to Rome.

FOLLOWING PAGES *The Death of Caesar shows the assassination of the great Roman emperor in 44 BCE. An oil painting by Guillaume Lethiere (1760–1832).*

The Second Civil War, 44–31 BCE

CHAPTER VI

O ur tyrant deserved to die. Here was a man who wanted to be king of the Roman people and master of the whole world. Those who agree with ambition like this must also accept the destruction of existing laws and freedoms. It is not right or fair to want to be king in a state that used to be free and ought to be free today.

Cicero on the assassination of Julius Caesar

The view expressed by Gaius Matius, a friend of Caesar's, is different, but equally Roman:

People blame me for mourning the death of my friend. They say my country should be preferred to my friends, as if they had proved that killing him was good for the state. I did not abandon him as a friend, however much I disapproved of what he was doing...

Here then are two views of the death of Julius Caesar. The one from Matius is a genuine and heartfelt affirmation of what friendship means. The other, from Cicero, is a judgment by someone who had known Caesar as a political enemy since he first came to speak in the Senate 24 years before.

Caesar was 56 years old when he died and, as Plutarch wrote, "the supreme power which he had pursued all his life and which he achieved left him but an empty name and a glory that made him envied by his fellow citizens. As for his murderers fate hounded them down and avenged his murder..."

OPPOSITE *The battle of Actium and the defeat of Antony and Cleopatra by the Roman navy under Agrippa (September 2, 31 BCE).*

Cicero, an experienced and angry politician, described the actions of the assassins as bungled. He believed that if they were going to root out corruption in government then they should have killed Mark Antony as well, although others, such as Marcus Junius Brutus, felt this was unnecessary.

Known in the past for his riotous living Antony was, even his enemies agreed, a brave man. However, Cicero believed that Antony was a weak man who did not realize his weakness yet thought he was as capable of ruling as Caesar. Cicero believed that men like Antony were the cause of great disasters, as they are given to compromise and are cruel and divisive in their actions. He believed that Antony was a man who was successful only when he was threatened.

But there was an unknown factor in the struggle to fill the power vacuum caused by Caesar's death—Octavian. Aged just 19, Octavian was studying Greek in Apollonia when Caesar was murdered. The young man had come to the attention of the former dictator when he delivered a funeral oration in honor of his grandmother Julia, who had been Caesar's sister. At 16 he joined the army and when Caesar went to fight Pompey's sons in Spain in 45 BCE, Octavian followed. He traveled with a small escort along enemy-infested roads, was shipwrecked and sick but pressed on to join Caesar. It was an act that pleased the dictator, who adopted Octavian as his heir in his will, having no legitimately born son of his own. With the death of his adoptive father, Octavian decided to return to Rome in order to claim his inheritance and take revenge against the assassins.

The Aftermath of Assassination

However, for the moment it was Mark Antony who was in the ascendant. But before we consider his actions, let us look at the immediate actions of the conspirators.

They had expected public acclamation. Instead, the people of Rome were incensed and took to the streets where one innocent man who was suspected of being involved in the murder was torn limb from limb. The conspirators had not believed that the people would be against them and hid. The day after the assassination they came down from hiding and Brutus made a speech to which the people listened in silence. Antony had arranged that a decree of amnesty for the killing would be passed by the Senate in an effort to reconcile all parties. He ensured that his fellow consul, Dolabella, and also Lepidus, who controlled the only troops in Rome, should be persuaded to side with the conspirators. Cicero believed that the Republic would return as the result of the dictator's death, but the Senate proclaimed that he was to be worshipped as a god. In attempting to temper the situation and bring all sides together Antony believed that everything would be resolved without more bloodshed and he would emerge as the natural successor to Caesar.

Five days after the assassination, the people of Rome heard the terms of Caesar's will. He left half of what he had to be divided between each Roman citizen. When the masses saw the mutilated body of their former leader being carried through the Forum, they tore down railings and benches and tables and made a pyre and burned the body. Then the angry people lit torches, went looking for the assassins and burned their houses. The conspirators went to ground and even Antony realized that the transition of power would not be as smooth as he would like, despite the fact that immediately after Caesar's death his deputy had gained the support of the masses and the army. Antony was entrusted with Caesar's papers and treasures by Calpurnia, his widow. He treated the conspirators with respect and passed measures to abolish dictatorship forever.

RIGHT *A marble bust by Canova of the young Octavian, who was the Emperor Augustus (63 BCE–14 CE).*

Street riots were severely put down and one of the ringleaders of the civil disorder, Amatius, was executed on Antony's orders. Antony was fool enough to believe that everything was his for the taking. He spent Caesar's wealth—Octavian's inheritance—in a wanton display of debauchery. But Antony reckoned without the will of Octavian. The young man demanded to know where the fortune Caesar had left him was and what Antony intended to do to make reparation for the money he had squandered.

Antony refused to welcome Octavian. He and many others believed that the boy could be easily outmaneuvered in the political power struggles that were imminent. On the other hand, the patrician Optimate Party, which was already afraid of Antony's ambitions, welcomed Octavian into the fold. Cicero and the Optimates believed that all they had to do with one so young was humor him until he could be dispensed with, but Octavian was not only ambitious, he also had great natural skills as a leader and a politician. Cicero and those ranged against him would find this truth to their cost. Octavian was not a man who was going to compromise when it came to the fate of Caesar's murderers. He wanted them to be tried and to receive justice—and if no one would apply the law then he would. Octavian had a pedigree that would daunt greater men than Antony or Cicero.

There was a story told of the young man lunching in a copse by the Appian Way. He was close to the fourth milestone and as he was eating an eagle swooped at him, snatched the crust from his hand and carried it high into the sky. Then, to his great surprise, the eagle glided gently down and restored what it had taken. Rome, the eagle, would be subservient to Octavian—he was clearly marked by the gods to be a great leader.

Marcus Junius Brutus and Cassius fled Italy for the east, leaving Antony in complete charge of the provinces. The Senate voted that Antony should be given the province of Gaul and the use of four of Caesar's legions. However, Decimus Brutus, another of the conspirators had been promised Gaul by Caesar, so he set about raising his own troops to take on Antony. Civil War was imminent and the battle lines began to be drawn.

Octavian understood that he had to move. He took command of Caesar's veterans in Campania. Two legions, the Martian and the IV, deserted Antony when they heard that Caesar's son was raising troops, such was the power of Caesar's name.

The Second Civil War Begins

In January 43 BCE the Second Civil War began when the Senate gave Octavian the title of senator and praetor, which made him the head of legal matters in Rome. Octavian, astutely, had already paid out of his personal fortune the legacies Caesar had promised to the people.

By now the war of words waged by Cicero against Mark Antony was in full flow. Cicero was a brave man—he had stood for certain political principals all his life and he refused to abandon them. He persuaded the Senate to name Mark Antony a public enemy.

Antony, knowing his troops could not be relied upon in any confrontation with Octavian, turned on Decimus Brutus in Cisalpine Gaul and crushed him. Then, in April 43 BCE Octavian's army met Antony and defeated him. Antony moved to Transalpine Gaul where Decimus Brutus pursued him. Decimus hoped for help from Lepidus but he did not receive it. Octavian left them to fight in a masterly stroke of inaction. At the same time, the Senate decided that Octavian was too great a threat to their power and they withdrew their support.

Meanwhile Cassius had taken command in Syria while Marcus Brutus took Macedonia. They wanted to unite to destroy Octavian and Antony. It was a vain hope. Octavian was consolidating his popularity.

The Second Triumvirate

In November, Antony, Octavian and Lepidus met and put aside their enmity to form the Second Triumvirate. Between them, they controlled 43 legions and agreed to carve up the Roman world. They came into power on a wave of terror, reminiscent of Sulla's rise to power. Senators and knights were killed on the mere suspicion of supporting the assassins of Caesar, opposing the Triumvirate or, often, because the Triumvirs wanted to take money. In December Antony insisted that his old enemy Cicero be slaughtered—the outspoken republican died bravely.

The Triumvirate looked east and marched on Brutus and Cassius. In 42 BCE, the Caesarians

ABOVE *The death of Brutus, who died on his own sword after the Battle of Philippi (42 BCE). Oil painting by Guerin.*

RIGHT *A marble bust of Agrippa, Roman general and military adviser to Emperor Augustus.*

and Republicans faced each other at the Battle of Philippi in Macedonia. The Republicans were defeated and both Cassius and Brutus died on their own swords.

Antony and Octavian divided their areas of interest. Antony took the eastern dominions, while Octavian was to have the most difficult assignment. He had to gain control of the Mediterranean islands and southern Italy and to keep the Roman veterans happy while controlling the western reaches of the empire.

The question of who would finally rule Rome would dog their promises and treaties. Antony was a lucky general and soldiers like a lucky leader. He was powerful, in his prime and experienced, while at only 21 Octavian was small and in delicate health. But Octavian had as his friend and adviser a low-born but powerful soldier, Marcus Vipsanius Agrippa.

Agrippa was Octavian's right-hand man for the rest of their lives. People began to remark on the diplomatic skills and ruthlessness of Octavian. He ensured that everything he did was part of an overall scheme. Nothing Octavian did was ever by chance.

In 40 BCE, Octavian's elder sister, Octavia, married Antony. For a time she protected Antony from his own excess. Octavian consolidated his power in Rome, a city that "he found [in] brick and left [in] marble." He distributed land among the veteran soldiers and organized work on the restoration and refurbishment of public buildings. He repressed all banditry in Italy and set up a police force in Rome to keep the citizens secure but also repressed.

Antony and Cleopatra

Antony first met the Egyptian queen, Cleopatra, in 41 BCE. He followed her to Egypt for a time, although his interests in Italy and the influence of Octavia kept him from her. From 39 BCE he lived in Athens with his wife, but in 37 BCE, he met up with Cleopatra and the two became lovers once more. Antony gave away Roman provinces in the east to her relatives like an oriental despot. He attacked Parthia in 36 BCE and invaded Armenia in 34 BCE By now, his relationship with Octavian was in tatters.

When he divorced Octavia in 32 BCE, Octavian cleverly declared war on Cleopatra rather than on Antony, which would have been divisive in Rome and for the Senate. Octavian managed to persuade the Romans that he was fighting for their religion, family life, honor and the survival of Rome itself against a whoring Egyptian queen.

On September 2, 31 BCE a Roman fleet commanded by Agrippa trapped Antony and Cleopatra's navy off Actium and destroyed it (see panel on facing page). Antony and Cleopatra fled to Egypt, where in 30 BCE Octavian followed with his army. Antony and Cleopatra made a desperate throw for power by pointing out that Caesarion was Caesar's real offspring and not simply an adopted son like Octavian.

It made no difference. Octavian and his legions defeated Antony, who killed himself. Cleopatra failed to charm Octavian and, refusing to become a slave in a Triumph in Rome, also committed suicide.

Antony, a man of 50, had abandoned ambition, wife and Rome for the Egyptian Queen. Rome now had one undisputed ruler who knew that to retain power he had to find ways to assure the people of Rome of his Republican sentiments. Octavian knew that it was only when he had achieved this that he could act as he wished and impose his rule over the Roman empire. The imposition of that power had to be subtle and discreet. What his great-uncle had wanted to achieve by force of arms, Octavian achieved by cunning and diplomatic skill. In 27 BCE, Octavian was honored with the name "Augustus," which meant divine. Augustus would rule Rome and the world for more than 40 years.

BELOW *A relief on Trajan's column showing ships of the type that fought at Actium (31 BCE).*

THE BATTLE OF ACTIUM

Suetonius reported a story about Octavian prior to the Battle of Actium: "Before the battle he was about to board his ship when he met a peasant driving an ass. [Octavian] asked him his name and the peasant told him it was 'Eutychus,' which means 'prosper' and the name of his ass was 'Nicon' which means 'victory.'"

Antony had wintered with his fleet in the vast bay called the Ambracian Gulf, which is almost shut off from the sea by the headland known as Actium. He had his army of 100,000 infantry and 12,000 cavalry as well as thousands of eastern auxiliaries there. When he discovered that Agrippa's fleet had moored across the mouth of the bay, he attempted to escape the bottleneck. It would be necessary to fight his way out when the time came. Antony was confident of success as he had huge superiority. He had 500 galleys—some of ten banks of oars—while Octavian's navy had half that number of much smaller boats and an army of about 80,000 infantry and 12,000 cavalry. It was the skill and genius of Agrippa that made Octavian's victory possible.

Antony sailed out of the gulf and faced the line of Octavian's ships. Agrippa sailed a host of fireships into Antony's lines, which instantly caused panic. Cleopatra's ships broke out of the bay and sailed for Egypt followed by Antony and what was left of his fleet. His army in the countryside around the bay surrendered to Octavian and Agrippa less than seven days later.

Suetonius reported that "To commemorate the victory Octavian set up bronze statues of the peasant and his ass ... called Nicon and created a sacred enclosure for them."

Augustus, the First Emperor, 27 BCE–14 CE

VII

CHAPTER

A T THE AGE OF 36 Augustus was experienced enough to know that he had to disguise the extent of his true power. Having defeated Antony, Lepidus, Sextus Pompeius, the son of Pompey, and Decimus Brutus in battle and taken revenge on those who had murdered Caesar, he was in a position in which no single institution of state nor any individual could stand against him. His acceptance of the name Augustus suggests that he was touched with a divine mission. The people of Rome had rejected monarchy over 200 years earlier. It would require subtlety and political skill to make the changes he was determined to make.

Augustus wrote that immediately after the Second Civil War "he transferred the State from his own authority to the control of the Senate and people of Rome." He sent this claim to the corners of the empire, although it was far from true. He wanted the people to believe that he was merely the first citizen among all citizens and that the offices he held had always been held by past leaders. The hidden nature of the control he wielded would gradually be stripped away by future emperors, but at the beginning of the age of the Roman Empire it was possible to maintain the illusion.

OPPOSITE *The Emperor Augustus with his staff of office and a thunderbolt signifying divinity. Stone, first century CE.*

Augustus held all the offices he took for life, while other officers of the state held them for limited periods. He agreed to govern all the frontier provinces, and by doing this, he took command of the entire Roman army and so could keep them loyal under the watch of officers of his own choosing. Augustus determined that this, the ultimate weapon of control, should be thoroughly professional—soldiers should have proper pay and conditions.

In theory Augustus and the Senate ruled in parallel—the Senate could make laws, Augustus could issue edicts; the Senate controlled the Roman treasury, Augustus managed the finances of the provinces; the Senate was the high court; Augustus could try important cases if he wished to. Augustus appeared to have increased the powers of the Senate, but in fact he had balanced them by increasing in his own powers. He had made the Senate subservient to the emperor.

Augustus controlled the membership of the Senate because he controlled the selection of candidates. He reduced its numbers and removed any low-born or foreign members. While the people also seemed to be governed as they had been before, Augustus controlled their elections too and legislation by the people's committees became rarer. Augustus realized that it was only essential to provide the people with entertainment and cheap corn to keep them quiet.

He improved the position of the equestrian class, making them officers in the provinces, suppliers for the armies, prefects in charge of corn supplies and managers of vast estates. He also passed to them the duty of controlling the police in the city, which connected them directly to him and reduced the influence of the Senate. Augustus insisted that provincial magistrates improved the great network of roads and also decreed that the slave population should live in comfortable conditions.

The period of relative stability that followed the Second Civil War enabled Augustus to oversee the distribution of land to his veterans. He was anxious to keep the army on his side. The armies on the German frontiers, which were commanded by Tiberius Claudius Nero and Nero Claudius Drusus, the sons of Augustus's wife Livia, became dissatisfied. They felt that being forced to serve for 20 years with the colors was too long. They wanted a 16-year commitment, pensions and land, as they had been promised in the past.

Augustus sent a senior officer to investigate the reasons for this unprecedented revolt. Some wanted to kill their superiors. When the investigating officer came into the camps old soldiers grabbed his hands and made him feel their toothless gums and look at their wounds and their tattered clothes. They stripped their shirts off and showed the bloody wounds on their backs that had been caused not by the enemy but by the whips and canes of their officers.

The investigating officer promised to bring their complaints to Augustus himself on the understanding that they would give up the leaders of the unrest. These men were sentenced to death for fomenting mutiny and were slaughtered.

Augustus also began to rebuild the physical infrastructure of the empire. Roads and forts were repaired and renewed and temples that had fallen into a ruinous state as a result of the decline of Roman religious observance were rebuilt. Those who wanted to gain favor with the emperor knew that all they had to do was to pay for the restoration of a temple. Augustus decreed that the institutions that had been built up during the Roman Republic should remain in place, but he also instigated changes that were essential to the smooth functioning of the empire. Augustus knew that the administration of such a vast domain could not remain in the hands of a self-electing and centralized group of Roman citizens. The Senate might have achieved greatness for the city, but controlling and legislating a territory that extended from modern Belgium to the Pyrenees, from Germany to Greece, from the Alps to North Africa and from Spain to Judaea needed local checks and balances that could be provided only by a properly organized civil service. Through this network he kept in close touch with all parts of the empire.

This new order determined that the control and governance of the entire empire would be fair and egalitarian. The law in Rome should have the same characteristics as the law in Gaul or Judaea. Justice should be administered in Rhodes in the same way as in Spain. Men or women accused of a crime in Macedonia should be able to expect the same from the court as a man or woman in Gaul. While the detail of systems might change as the emperors came and went, it was under Augustus that such methods of enforcing imperial control were laid down. Augustus created a climate in which political change was

LEFT *A frieze from the Arc of Peace, which was consecrated in 9 BCE, marking the return of Augustus from campaigns in Gaul and Spain.*

BELOW *A marble statue of the Empress Livia Drusilla, wife of Augustus.*

appropriate to all. It was a magnificent balancing act and he managed to sustain it until the end of his reign.

Augustus knew that the patricians in powerful political and social positions felt that their wealth, ambition, power and the framework by which they lived had to be protected. He knew that they would resist any attempt to take away what they regarded as their rightful place in the hierarchy. They were right to be suspicious of his motives but there was little or nothing they could do to oppose them.

Augustus was a man in touch with all levels of the Roman community. Farmers, statesmen, freemen and members of the far empire all believed he heard their grievances and, indeed, through his civil servants, he very often did. If he felt it was to his advantage, he would act on what he heard. He had an air that charmed many who met him. He concealed his power behind a ready smile and used simple and direct language when he spoke or addressed meetings.

Sulla's determination to impose his will on the city years earlier had destroyed the resistance of the people. Augustus built on this by presenting a much more sympathetic image. For nearly half a century, Augustus guarded his power jealously. He prepared for the succession and ensured that the role of emperor was hereditary. He was determined that the rulers of Rome would no longer be created by the Senate.

Family Life

Augustus married Antony's stepdaughter, Claudia, who was just of marriageable age, to cement his brief alliance with Antony but divorced her soon after. Then he married Scribonia who had been married twice before to consuls. She bore Augustus his only legitimate child, Julia. According to Suetonius he divorced Scribonia in 39 BCE "because [he] could not bear the way she nagged [him]." He took Livia Drusilla from her husband, despite the fact that she was pregnant at the time, and they remained together until he died. In 2 BCE, he banished his daughter Julia to a remote island for immorality. He had a puritanical zeal when it came to the behavior of members of his family, despite the fact that he took his own pleasures where he wanted.

Augustus was not greedy and even his homes were not ostentatious by the standards of the time. He was a man of simple tastes, but was also a man of great personal vanity. Suetonius wrote:

Augustus liked to believe that his eyes shone with a sort of divine radiance and it gave him deep pleasure if anyone at whom he glanced should drop their eyes as though dazzled by looking into the sun. By old age he had only partial vision in one eye, his teeth were small and few and decayed,

ABOVE *The three-tiered Pont du Gard crossing the River Gard as it takes water from Uzes to Nîmes in France.*

ears of moderate size and hair yellowish and curly. He was short but beautifully proportioned...

Augustus suffered from ill health and was rather superstitious, he often talked about his dreams with soothsayers and philosophers whom he invited to meet him from time to time.

A Golden Age

The reign of Augustus was an age when ideas, books, architecture, poetry and drama flourished. Horace, Virgil, Ovid, Seneca, and Propertius were contemporary writers and magnificent buildings like the Pont du Gard, the Arch of Augustus and the Theater of Marcellus were all built during this period.

Augustus encouraged writers by attending their plays and hearing them read their poems and books. It is said that two years after commissioning Virgil to write a poem about the fall of Troy and the founding of Rome he asked the poet to show him what he had written. A fearful Virgil admitted reluctantly that there was

nothing to show. Augustus was not angry and Virgil continued to enjoy Augustus's generosity until the time came when he could read the first books of *The Aeneid* to the emperor.

Lasting Power

Caesar had not bothered to conceal his contempt for the Senate. Augustus and his successor, Tiberius, knew that the pretense that the Senate had power was necessary to ensure that power truly continued to reside in one man. Augustus wanted the power to last beyond his time and he set about ensuring that it did.

To base an empire on the lie that the people still held the reins was dangerous, but when Augustus died he passed on an empire that was secure at home and on its frontiers. Augustus used the age-old tactic of divide and rule—he flattered tribal leaders with gifts of Roman citizenship; he included the most bellicose tribes into the Roman army as paid auxiliaries and built roads and bridges that benefited both Romans and the conquered tribes.

Augustus advised Tiberius not to extend the empire further into Germany. Germany might be a province nominally, but the legions wintered on the Gallic side of the Rhine. It was not until 4 CE that Tiberius first dared to winter on the German bank of the Rhine for the tribes were fiercely warlike and made uneasy neighbors.

Augustus claimed to be running a nation based on the old values of Roman life—the family, codes of morality and religion, and the traditional values of law, peace and order. He continually made it clear that his decisions had a firm legal base. He claimed there was continuity between the ancient systems of Roman society and the system

he advocated. The balance he kept between the illusion and the reality was a magnificent feat of statesmanship.

In 14 CE, Augustus died. On his deathbed he did not linger: "Goodbye Livia, never forget our marriage," were his last words. Shortly afterwards he was declared "divine," and a cult developed around him. After his death, the frontiers of the Roman Empire remained virtually static, apart from the conquest of Britain, which was completed by Claudius in 43 CE. It is true that between 101–117 CE Trajan acquired vast new territory, but it all reverted to its previous status after he died.

BELOW *Virgil reading his epic* The Aeneid *to Augustus, Augustus's wife Livia and his sister Octavia. Nineteenth-century oil painting by Ingres.*

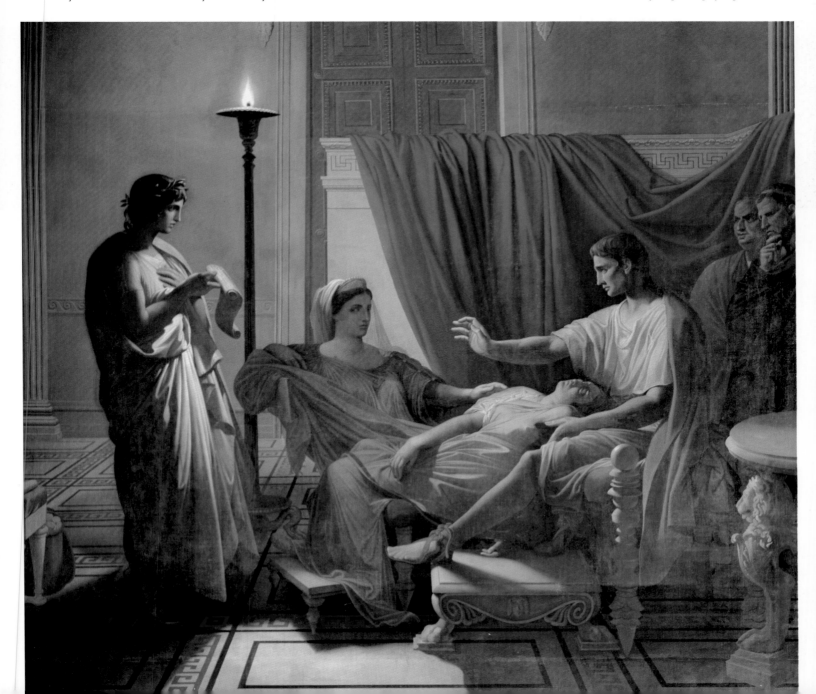

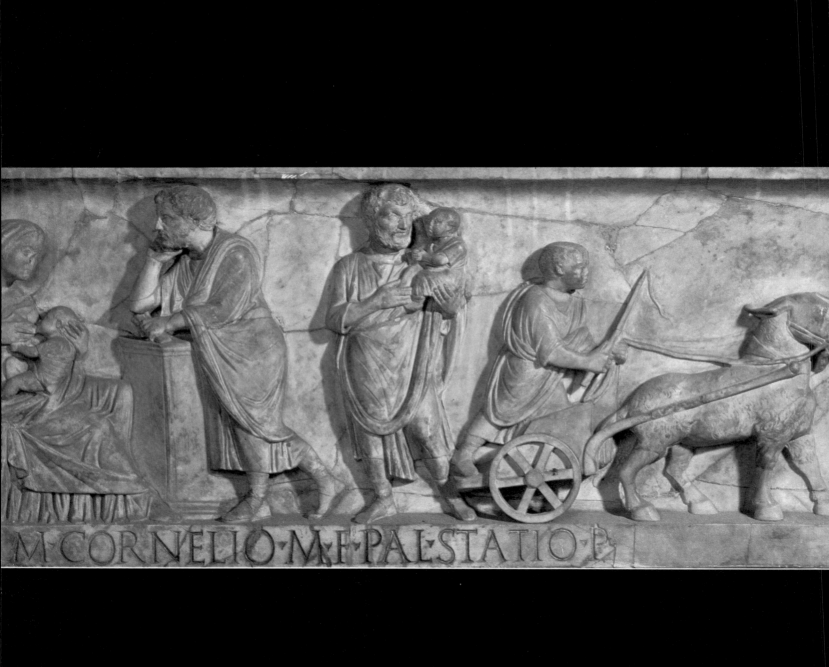

M·CORNELIO·M·F·PAL·STATIO·P·

The Roman Way of Life

VIII

IN MANY WAYS life in ancient Rome was the forerunner of the best and the worst of modern society. At the time of Julius Caesar the city was a jumble of apartment blocks known as *insulae* that consisted of three or four rickety floors. These buildings were interconnected by a chaos of narrow alleys and streets that made Rome a dangerous city, particularly at night. The villas of the rich were set apart or were sometimes built in the ground floor of such blocks.

The Streets

The poet Juvenal (*c* 55–130 CE) complained that "walking down a street meant walking through filth." The streets of Rome were incredibly dirty underfoot and usually just wide enough for two people to pass. During his reign, Julius Caesar banned all carts and wagons from the streets from dawn to dusk—if he hadn't, it would have been impossible for the citizens of the city to go about their business. But this meant that the nights were packed with the grinding of wagon wheels and the cries of the drivers as they supplied the markets for morning. According to Juvenal sleep was impossible; he reported that "the crossing of wagons in the narrow winding streets, the swearing of drovers in traffic jams would snatch sleep from a sea cow or the emperor himself."

OPPOSITE *A relief from a marble sarcophagus showing scenes from a child's life.*

RIGHT *A long street in Pompeii indented with the grooves caused by the passing of chariots and carts.*

By dawn the streets were packed with pedestrians pushing through the crowd. Men carrying scaffolding poles and beams for never-ending building works were a menace, but the city was expanding and building had to go on. A wine merchant carrying a wine cask might drop it, curse and watch the wine drain away into the filth at his feet. Nothing stopped in this hustling city.

Rome grew by the day with cheap houses being built for the flood of workers being thrown off the land, new temples, baths, drainage systems, the footings for new aqueducts and marble and mosaic floors to furnish the villas of the rich. It was a remarkable expansion.

The streets near the markets were filled to bursting with produce. A metalworker in a dark workshop might suddenly plunge iron into a fire and sparks would fly from the room into the daylight. Small tables set up against walls were loaded with herbs and spices from all over the empire: saffron; pepper; huge lumps of dried salt from the sea or the salt lakes in Greece, Cyprus or Africa; paprika; marjoram; garlic; fish paste; harissa; and fragrant grasses all added their scents to the morning air.

Shops spilled into the streets, regardless of imperial orders. Cooking pots and pans, lamps, piles of fruit and vegetables lay everywhere. Men from Syria, Egypt, or Spain called and beckoned to show what they had for sale. Soldiers from the legions and auxiliaries from distant lands watched. Slaves crowded around market stalls to buy meat, vegetables, fresh fish and fruit for their masters.

Gold was hammered into bracelets and earrings. Meat and fish were cooked over fires and black wine was poured into wine skins from huge barrels brought in from the countryside. Beggars demanded alms or showed rotting stumps and told of heroic deeds as soldiers. And there was always the press of men pushing into the market to barter, to trade, to buy and to sell. Storytellers from Asia sat in the shade of umbrellas, awaiting a listener for their tales. This was Rome in the daytime. It was an exciting and almost a magical place. At night it was different.

Little moonlight could edge into the narrow, stinking streets. Neither light nor sign marked the way. If a man went to dinner with friends he would, if he was sensible, take a house slave for protection or pay the neighborhood watchmen to escort him. Juvenal, half mockingly, wrote that anyone who walked alone in the streets without making a will was a careless man.

Eventually the city settled into silence with

ABOVE *Stone relief of a stallholder offering fruit and vegetables for sale in an open-air market.*

ABOVE *The aqueduct at Segovia, Spain, bringing water from the distant snow-capped mountains into the city.*

AQUEDUCTS

Inevitably rivers such as the Tiber were polluted. The Romans knew that adequate supplies of fresh, clean water were a protection against outbreaks of illness. According to some accounts, fresh water arrived in ancient Rome via eight aqueducts, which fed the public conduits, basins and fountains used by the city's inhabitants. The water was used for drinking, washing and cleaning the public lavatories. This technology spread across the empire making fresh, clean water available to most citizens. Only the wealthy had private water supplies.

The water transported by aqueducts came across great distances from fresh water springs along stone-built causeways and drains. These magnificent feats of engineering provided water wherever it was needed. The Romans realized that water had to flow at a slow and steady pace and conduits were built on shallow slopes. They even solved the problem of making water run uphill—forcing water into the narrow end of a stone funnel puts it under pressure and allows it to travel up a slight incline.

By 97 CE the aqueducts that fed in to Rome were designed by Sextus Julius Frontinus. His system fed around 1,000 million liters a day to the city. Frontinus wrote: "compare this with the idle pyramids and the useless, if famous, buildings of Greece."

windows shut, gates barred and the citizens asleep. Then the carts and wagons of the farmers rolled in and it began again. The rumble of carts, the clatter of hooves, the murmur of beasts going to their slaughter, men wrapped against the fog, mist and the cold already making bargains in the shadows. And women looking for clients. Cities don't change so much even after 2,000 years.

Rome's poor lived in the overcrowded, insanitary apartment blocks that had few of the benefits of this emerging civilization. These blocks were unhygienic, unlit and the corridors were congested with people and their belongings. Water was transported by aqueducts (see panel on the facing page) and supplied public taps, public baths and washhouses.

The Plebeians

Life for the poor was not easy. Some found work as casual laborers while others were craftsmen or tradesmen. Cobblers, butchers, dressmakers, leather workers and other tradesmen lived above their shops. After a brief breakfast they would be at work. Their wives often worked alongside them while looking after their children.

Those with no trade could find irregular work on building sites or in the markets. Some carried drinking water in huge jars or skins to sell where they could, while others ran errands, carried messages and generally ducked and dived to scrape a living.

The working day was short, usually finishing at about midday. This left the afternoons and the nights free for entertainment. It has been calculated that there were over 100 days a year set aside for public holidays, anniversaries, religious festivals, official games and such like. Idle people needed to be entertained or trouble might erupt.

Rome was a magnet for the people in the countryside. These incomers added to the city's vast, expanding population and put pressure on those in charge to provide work and housing. Families and servants, workers and apprentices lived cheek by jowl. Verminous rooms were a permanent source of disease. Disease was feared, but most feared of all was fire.

If a fire took hold in one of these wood, plaster and stone tenements a whole district would be in danger. Rome had its own fire brigade, but no warnings or rules could prevent fire breaking out from time to time. Some Romans, like Caesar's friend Crassus, made money out of fire (see panel).

FIRE

Marcus Licinius Crassus, one of the richest men in Rome, built his fortune chasing fires. If a fire broke out he rushed to the site to offer the owner sympathy, before offering to buy the smoldering ruins and the land, all too often for a pitiful price. The owner was usually only too pleased to be rid of it. Crassus meanwhile brought in a team of builders to build a new block, which he then rented out at a good profit.

The best housing was for those who could afford separate villas, which were often magnificent (see panel, page 90).

Domestic life

Rome woke at dawn and the daily routine was austere. The master of the house would rise and dress in a short tunic and a large linen square called a toga, which he wore around his body and draped over one shoulder. Togas had a colored border that denoted the wearer's social position.

ABOVE *A shoemaker sits astride his bench mending a shoe on a wooden last. Relief from a stone sepulchre.*

THE ROMAN VILLA

ABOVE *Hadrian's villa was a traditional Roman country house built at Tivoli, 117–138 CE.*

The villa was a single-story building built around a pillared central hall called an atrium. A covered corridor resembling a medieval cloister connected the roofed rooms that opened into this passageway. In the center of the house there was often a secluded and shady garden. Rooms off the atrium and the garden were decorated with plaster on which an artist might have painted a formal picture.

If the villa was owned by a very wealthy family a mosaic maker was sometimes employed to create a design that represented a story from Greek or Roman myth. Often these were built into pools so that the colors of the stones remained bright. Mosaics were made by drawing a design into a cement base and then inlaying thousands of pieces of carefully cut stones. Each stone had a flat, colored surface. It was expensive and very skilled work.

Furniture was simple and functional with reclining couches, stools and low tables in the living areas. Beds were sprung on leather straps and were also simple. Water was often fed into villas by a system of lead or clay pipes and was used for washing and drinking. It could also be transported through an underfloor heating system known as a hypocaust (see opposite). It was the duty of domestic slaves to keep the system clean and to make sure that the water was heated when it was needed.

Villas needed large numbers of slaves to clean, cook and provide security. Often the master of the house provided quarters for a clerk and even a schoolmaster both of whom might be educated men from Greece or Alexandria but slaves nonetheless.

The master of the house then took his breakfast— one of three or four regular meals a day—while giving instructions about the household to his majordomo. This most trusted of slaves had his master's complete confidence and might even gain his freedom as a mark of respect and gratitude from the family on his owner's death.

Slaves cleaned the rooms while the gardener watered and tended the plants in the inner garden. The cook, a most important slave, checked the quality of the meat and fish that had been bought from the market.

It was time for the master's work to begin. In the street a barber cut his hair and shaved him, which was hazardous and often resulted in cuts and nicks. The best remedy to stop bleeding was said to be a spider's web soaked in oil and vinegar.

Meanwhile, back in the house, the lady of the house ate breakfast and, with the help of her personal slave, dressed her hair, applied such make-up as she wanted and dressed. Women wore the stola, a long linen tunic with gold stitching around the hem, tied with a belt and accompanied by a square cloak, which was often of a bright color. As the empire expanded, a rich woman's clothes also became more luxurious and silk and cotton might well take the place of wool and linen.

The mistress of the house made sure that the slave girls had taken the clothes and linen from the bedroom and that it was being washed. She instructed the cook as to whether there were guests for dinner in the evening or whether a simple meal was all that was needed.

The mistress might speak to the slave-tutor about the progress her son was making with his lessons. Then she and the majordomo would meet to discuss anything that needed attention. He was as much a key member of the household for her as for her husband. It is recorded that some slaves, who were often well-educated and cultured Greek or Egyptian prisoners of war, became the lovers of their owners' wives.

The mistress of a rich household had little more to do than to walk, attended by a slave girl, to visit a jeweler's shop or to sit spinning in the garden with her daughters, perhaps to discuss their betrothals, as they were often engaged at the age of 12. Later a rich woman might visit friends and go with them to the reserved part of the public baths (see panel on the facing page) to gossip and to have a massage. Then, before dusk she would be escorted home to wait for her husband's return.

ROMAN BATHS

The baths became a part of everyday life in the Roman Empire. Spas with natural hot springs became a focus for large complexes of buildings and if spas were not available huge public bathhouses were built around the cities of the empire and were fed with water from the aqueducts.

The buildings were an elegant focus for the inhabitants of cities such as Rome, Pompeii, Bath, Alexandria or Nîmes. Taking a bath was no simple matter; in the city of Bath there were three separate baths. A building of this complexity would have required fine engineering. First the building itself had to be attractive. Pillars lined an elegant cloister into which a large communal bath was sunk.

ABOVE *A collection of toilet and writing utensils. Ivory combs and scrapers, pens and a mirror stand. First century CE.*

Water was piped into this bath through many lead pipes, which were often decorated with mythic figures. It was heated in a tank by wood-burning furnaces and then led through a system of channels and pipes known as hypocausts into the baths.

The baths in Rome used over 400 miles (640 km) of aqueducts. In the late third century AD the baths of the Emperor Diocletian (240–313 CE) were the size of a modern soccer field and contained mosaics, massive marble columns and even statues of gods and emperors.

In Bath the hot springs provided a million liters of hot water every day at a temperature of around 48°F. Some Romans felt that such springs were sacred and threw in valuable objects to please the gods.

The system applied to using a public bath was the same throughout the empire. For a small fee a customer stripped and handed his clothes to an attendant. He then moved to an exercise ground to work out and build up a sweat. Then he moved to the bathing area. The first bath taken was called the *frigidairium* and was cold. After this the customer could exercise some more and having worked up a further sweat he would recline in the *tepidarium*—a warm bath. After time there he would finally move into the hot bath, the *caldarium*, which acted very much like a modern sauna. The baths provided a social focus as well as a means of keeping clean.

In baths like those in Pompeii there was a gymnasium. There were also masseurs in attendance to pound and pummel the customers. Having rubbed olive oil into a customer's skin they would then scrape it off with an instrument called a *strigli*. The masseur would then smooth sweet-smelling oils into the skin.

In 50 CE, the playwright Seneca wrote:

I live over a public bath-house. Can you imagine every sort of annoying noise? The fat gentleman does his exercise with lead weights; when he is working out, or pretending to, I can hear him grunt. When he breaths out I can hear him panting in a squeaking voice. Or some lazy fellow is happy with a cheap rub down and I hear the sound of the masseur's hand slapping his flesh.

THE FORUM

ABOVE *A wall painting from Pompeii thiat was a sign showing where to find the association of skilled woodworkers.*

The Forum was the focus of public and private business in any Roman city, and initially it was also a cattle market and place to shop. Porticos, pillars and a covered area provided shelter and shade for those who did daily business there. For a long time the Forum was where funeral games and contests were staged and religious ceremonies were performed. Temples were often established close to the Forum to accommodate religious rites. As Rome grew and habits changed, so did the Forum.

By 179 BCE many of the older characteristics of the Forum had moved to other sites. The religious aspects did remain, although public worship was observed less often. By the time of Julius Caesar, the Forum was too small to conduct all public and private business. In 107 CE Emperor Trajan (53–117 CE) began to construct the final magnificent site of the Forum. It was 300 feet (100 meters) long and 240 feet (80 meters) wide. The building had a huge portico that was supported by colonnades of pillars. Along the sides of the building were many small rooms, often with signs outside, that formed the headquarters of the associations or guilds of skilled workers from around the Roman Empire.

OPPOSITE *Men about to settle down to a banquet as a servant brings a finger bowl and another takes off one of the diner's shoes. Second century BCE.*

The richest men were the lawyers and the Senators who ruled the city or the knights of the equestrian class, whose interests lay in administration and trading. They were the bureaucrats, the wealthy landowners, the state officials and civil servants. Their world revolved around the Senate and the Forum (see panel).

A Gentleman's Afternoon

Work having finished, another brief meal, often of bread and fruit and cheese, was taken and the wealthy men of Rome were at leisure. They might take walks together, play games, meet friends or gossip just as their female counterparts did. Gambling was forbidden by the Senate, but it eventually became a terrible vice in the city. Juvenal wrote that men gambled recklessly: "Is it not mad to lose a fortune and not even have a shirt to give to a naked slave?" he asked.

Young men were expected to attend military training in the afternoons, rather than waste their time and energy on gambling and women. It was at this time of day that public games would begin.

The Evening Meal

At nightfall, public entertainment ended. If the master of the house was at home and had no guests, dinner was very simple and took little time to eat or to prepare. For both the rich and the less well off a normal dinner did not include much meat. The Romans used vegetables, herbs and spices, which were often accompanied by wheat flour porridge. If, on the other hand, a rich man was serving a banquet anything exotic that could be found in the market would be brought to the table.

Couches surrounded the low table and guests reclined on them to eat. Slaves entered with iced and perfumed water to wash the guests' hands before they ate. Then the food was served from huge bowls and platters. Wine was passed around in prodigiously large amounts.

The Romans were fond of spiced food and rich and spicy sauces. The domestic servants would prepare the sauces from vinegar and honey, pepper, and even old fish waste. These sauces would be added to chicken, duck, pigeon, ostrich, swan, crocodile, larks' tongues, boars' heads, peacocks, sturgeon, salmon and whatever else the market offered.

THE PUBLIC GAMES

After the unrest of the civil wars and an influx of citizens into the already overloaded city, the threat to good order was clear. The poor and unemployed had to be kept docile. Bread and circuses became the order of the day. By 50 BCE, there were approximately 130 days of holiday each year.

The games were not yet the full-blown orgy of death and killing that were frequently seen at the Colosseum at the time of Nero and Caligula. Initially, entertainment was mainly provided by horse and chariot racing, in which various teams competed against each other in reckless races. The people were entertained and free bread ensured that they were fed.

The games were given in the name of various gods and sacrifices were made before they began. During the era of the Kingdom a horse race would take place to celebrate the return of the army from its spring campaign. The winning horse was sacrificed to purify the city by shedding its blood and its skeleton was preserved to protect the city. In a similar way the autumn races saw the winning horse beheaded, its blood collected and some offered as a libation on the altar of Regia. "Blood poured on the ground to calm the god of death in heaven," said Ausonius. It was a dark portent of what was to come.

The people came in thousands to the amphitheater known as the Vallis Murcia, which later became the circus. It was 2,000 feet (610 meters) long and 625 feet (190 meters) wide. There was a spine down the center and wooden seats for the spectators were erected along the sides. Chariots were released simultaneously onto the track from starting stalls. A low wall protected spectators as the chariots hurtled around the track seven times. The noise and spectacle and the sight of their rulers sharing their excitement was enough to keep the people happy.

These races grew into other spectacles as time went by. The circus was adapted to accommodate other spectacles too. There were hunts in which tigers, lions, and other wild beasts were killed by armed men. Ditches around the circus were filled with water to prevent the wild animals escaping into the crowd.

Augustus was forced to make the games more and more exotic. The mob became more and more eager for blood. The people demanded that their ruler was as involved as they were. For example, when Julius Caesar came to the games and was clearly too bored to watch, they were not pleased. By showing his boredom he divorced himself from the people he ruled.

The racing and the spectacle provided a safety valve against revolution. The people were bought off by the games and increasingly fantastic sums of money were spent on them by the emperor and by those looking for political advancement.

ABOVE *Horse racing and chariot racing at the Circus Maximus. Stone relief from the first century CE.*

A favorite recipe consisted of dormice stuffed with minced pork, or the meat of another dormouse with chopped nuts, herbs, and pine nuts. It was cooked in a small oven and then dipped in honey and poppy seeds. These banquets might last as long as four or five hours and the guests, all men, would eat and drink until they could eat and drink no more.

Education

In the families of the wealthy, boys were educated and girls learned how to become good wives. In the families of the poor the children helped with the grinding work of the small farm or learned the skills of their father, for example as a cobbler, a butcher, a farrier, or a weapon maker.

In poor families baby girls were sometimes left on the town garbage piles to die. Parents of such children knew they would never be able to afford a dowry and that she would just be a financial drain on the family.

A boy would be educated at home if the family kept a well-educated slave to serve as a teacher. Whether the education was at home or in the back room of a local shop, the regime was harsh and punishment was cruel and unending. Beatings were routine, whether for late attendance, for making a mistake while reciting a poem or conjugating verbs. Boys were even held down across a chair to make a punishment more savage. Tears were not expected. Roman boys grew up to be able to take harsh punishment without a murmur. Everything was learned by heart and no questions were expected. If a teacher declared that a thing was so, then it was so … to ask why or how was to invite another beating.

Up to the age of 12, boys learned how to read and write and to do basic math. They used an abacus for math and a wax tablet and a stylus to write. If the father was liberal, he might allow his daughter to join these lessons. After the age of 12 boys learned about the writings of the philosophers and ideas of Roman authors. They also learned the art of public speaking, which for a patrician boy was essential in adult public life. In the later years of the Roman Empire a young man might make a tour of its various regions, traveling to Greece, Asia Minor, or Rhodes to study at the feet of teachers there.

Girls, on the other hand, had no further education unless they were fortunate in their father. They learned sewing, cooking and maybe how to play a musical instrument. A girl was the

BELOW *A stone relief panel of a school in which the teacher, probably a Greek slave, is instructing three boys.*

chattel of her father and he could do as he wished with her. Her best hope was an arranged marriage that was happy.

Marriage

Because the family was so important to the Romans, marriage was a very serious act. A girl might be as young as 12 and the groom only two years older. Their responsibility was the honorable continuation of the family name. Marriage was a situation that could not be left to the fancies of love, but was a matter for the head of the family. Choice was dictated by political and financial interests. A betrothal was formal, sacrifice was made and rings were exchanged if the soothsayer's reading was favorable.

All their friends were expected to witness the betrothal, the exchange of rings, and the signing of the contract declaring the amount of dowry the girl would bring. It also regulated other aspects like the period of betrothal. If the man had not married her within an agreed time she was free to marry another; if either broke the vows the girl was regarded as an adulteress and the boy risked a large fine as well as being considered a bigamist if he was betrothed again.

On the evening before the marriage the girl gave her dolls to the house gods of her father's house. Childhood was over; she put on a white tunic tied at the waist, she was veiled and sometimes wore flowers in her hair. The ceremony was a simple joining of hands by an elderly woman of proven virtue at the bride's house. At a banquet provided by her father they waited for the evening star to appear and the girl was taken in procession to her groom's house. Friends and relations attended, musicians played and the songs became more bawdy while the groom threw packets of money or nuts to the children for luck and fertility. The bride garlanded the door of the house with flowers and smeared the lintel with oil and was then carried into the house by two of the groom's friends. And so to the bed and to the consummation of the marriage.

A bride was owned by her husband.

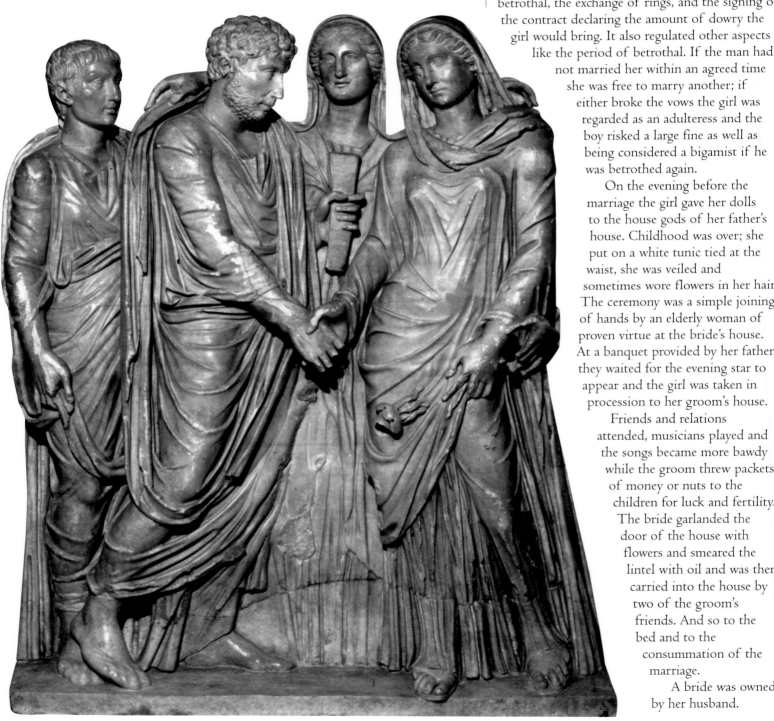

However, under Augustus the position of women changed. They were allowed to run a business and own property, and women, particularly of the patrician classes, began to gain their freedom. It was not long before it became impossible for a father to demand that a daughter marry a man and shift into a family of his choosing if she was unwilling.

Religion

Worship in Rome was centered on the gods who held particular responsibility for the seasons or the sun, the sky, war, the home, love or healing. The practice of religion was simple and animals were sacrificed in the temple to a particular deity. Mercury, Neptune, Mars, Venus, Vesta and Janus all had dedicated temples around the city and across the empire. At home the senior male in the house acted as priest for the family. At the entrance to each home was a cupboard containing a small shrine. Inside were the silver statuettes and symbols of household gods. Men or women leaving or returning to the house might pray to one of the household gods for a successful outcome of a journey or as thanks for a good day.

Priests were appointed by the Senate. As fathers could be the family priest, men like Julius Caesar could be designated as a priest on a wider

scale. He would be expected to help with the costs of the helpers, of the sacrifices and of the upkeep of a temple and would also take part in the conduct of the rituals. Often temples were built at great expense by wealthy public figures or by the emperor. Painted and gilded interiors, tall columns and images of the god to whom the temple was dedicated filled the building.

Men or women known as augurs were often attached to the temples. They could predict the future from studying the entrails of a sacrificed animal. Such predictions were taken very seriously by most Romans, but public worship became, as time went on, of less importance than the worship of the household gods.

Life in the Future

After decades of fighting, civil war and political unrest the city emerged as a stable and peaceful place to inhabit. The history of Rome began with fear: fear of hunger, fear of neighboring tribes, fear of non-Romans and fear, above all, of the barbarians on the distant frontiers. Some also feared the mighty Roman legions who spread across the known world and held back those frontiers. While they did that Rome was safe. Once the army lost confidence in its rulers, all would fly out of control.

ABOVE *A magnificent bull is brought for sacrifice to Mars, the god of war. Libations are poured at the altar.*

An Empire Built on Slavery

CHAPTER IX

SLAVES AND THEIR LABOR played a vital part in the economy of most regions in the ancient world, but of all the societies who used slaves, the Romans demonstrated a disregard for their treatment that was so callous that only the Etruscans emulated it. From the earliest history of the city to the end of the Roman Republic, slaves could expect little mercy and almost no consideration for their human needs. They were ruthlessly exploited by their owners and worked into early graves. Some historians estimate that the average age of a slave at death was just twenty-two.

At one time as many as a quarter of the men and women of the Roman Empire had no rights whatsoever. They did not even own themselves. They could be bought and sold at a whim; punished by being whipped, starved or beaten; or even crucified or killed in some other appalling manner if the owner wished. Slaves had no recourse to law as they were beyond the legal process. They labored at the bidding of a master or mistress. In most cases there was no concern for their feelings for, in the eyes of their owners, these simply did not exist. &

OPPOSITE *A slave woman combing a young girl's hair while others wait their turn. A fresco from Herculaneum, first century CE.*

FORTUNATA

We know of Fortunata because the British Museum holds a wax copy of the record of her sale in Londinium (London). Because of her lowly position we know very little more about Fortunata than that she was a slave. We have no record of her parents or of the person who bought her or of what she did for her owner.

How did a girl like Fortunata come to stand naked on the slave block in a market place in Londinium waiting for someone to look her over, check her for defects, look at her teeth as if she were a horse, check her arms and legs, her breasts and hair? She was probably a prisoner of war, perhaps from Gaul. A soldier may have taken her as part of his loot, or perhaps a general was asked to supply a slave dealer when he next defeated a Gallic tribe. Prospective buyers would have been allowed to touch her flesh, make her turn this way and that, and treat her as if she were no more than an animal. A pretty young boy would be treated in the same way. He would also fetch a high price, as did young Fortunata.

Fortunata was not more than 18 when she was sold. According to the tablet on which her sale was recorded she was purchased around 80–120 CE for 600 denarii, which was much more than a legionary soldier was paid for a year's service. Why was her price so high? It may be that she had a particular talent. If she was a skilled cook she might rise to a position of trust and power in a patrician household. Maybe she was a hairdresser. Maybe she could spin and weave. Or maybe she was beautiful and caught the eye of the man who paid for her—she may have been his concubine until he grew bored and tired of her only to sell her again at the same slave market. Apart from her brief appearance on a receipt, Fortunata's fate is unknown. We can only hope she was lucky and went to work in a decent household.

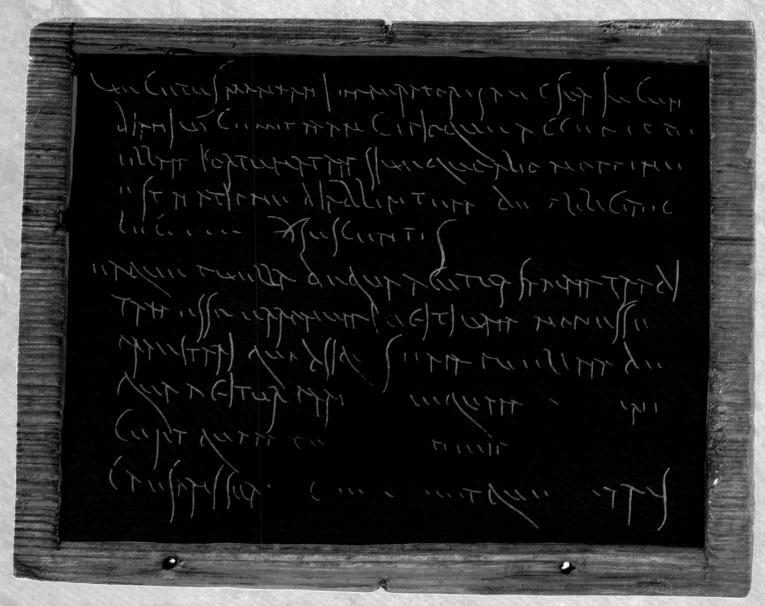

ABOVE *Wax copy of the deed of sale of the slave girl Fortunata.*

Slaves flooded into the empire as a result of Roman conquests in other lands. As Rome colonized the Greek city states of southern Italy and the lands owned by Carthage, the number of available slaves grew dramatically. From about 300 BCE slaves poured into Rome, sent by victorious generals to be sold in their name on the city's slave blocks. Fortunes were made as a result of the slave trade. The numbers of individuals involved are astonishing: 30,000 were enslaved at Tarentum in 272 BCE and 75,000 slaves came onto the market as a result of the First Punic War (see page 21) alone. In 167 BCE 150,000 slaves came from Epirus and in 101 BCE the same number were transported from Germany, while Caesar's wars in Gaul supplied as many as 500,000 serfs to Rome and other markets around the Mediterranean.

Apart from being captured as a prisoner of war, there were other ways that an individual could be forced into slavery. Men, women and children could be enslaved by law. Debt was a major contributor to the masses of slaves that populated both the cities and rural areas. The first table of Roman laws—the Twelve Tables—were written in about 449 BCE and stated that the punishment for debt was slavery. The result of this statute meant that, in some cases, debtors were condemned to pay off what they owed by becoming the slave of the person to whom they owed money.

The offspring of impoverished families were also vulnerable to slavery. The baby daughters of poor families were sometimes abandoned, as they would prove to be a financial burden. If anyone took in such a foundling, she automatically became that person's slave and was owned for life. It was also not uncommon for the father of a poor family to sell off his older sons to raise money. If they had been trained as carpenters, brick-makers, shepherds, or plowmen, they could command a high price for their skills. They were also young enough to provide work for a number of years and so they were seen as a good investment. In some countries that became part of the empire, kings and tribal chiefs sold off their most troublesome subjects to Roman generals. In this way they made a profit and might be relieved of a domestic problem.

Regular huge increases in the availability of slave labor were caused by unemployment among the peasant farmers whose land was taken over by wealthy city dwellers and property owners. These dispossessed farmers had no other skills and gravitated to the cities where they inevitably became an impoverished underclass.

On the vast farms owned by absentee landlords who inhabited the cities of the Roman Empire the work was almost always undertaken by slaves. There was a ready supply of human labor and it was not unusual for oxen to be better fed and housed than the humans who worked in the fields. The absentee landlords revelled in the vast profits to be made from their huge properties. Grain for the city, fruit, vegetables and meat were all produced by the labor of men and women who were kept in slave barracks and worked under the lash until they dropped.

In about 160 BCE, Marcus Porcius Cato (234–149 BCE) wrote a book called *On Agriculture* in which he made it quite clear that his interest was only in making a profit. He treated his animals better than the slaves because animals didn't know how to look after themselves. In his view slaves should be chained in dungeons when not working. But the slaves' overseer should not be vindictive. Cato wrote: "When at home a slave has to be either at work or asleep."

Cato liked the sleepy ones the best, as they were ready for more work after rest. The matter of sex was resolved by allowing his male slaves to use

ABOVE *Inside a Roman kitchen where slaves are preparing food. This is a relief from the country outside the city, c. 250 BCE.*

the little money they may have been given by guests or for doing good work to buy the use of a female slave from time to time. If any slave showed a skill for training younger slaves, Cato lent him money to teach them and then kept the newly trained slave for himself while crediting the slave trainer by commanding the best price available for him.

Apart from the mine workers and the farm slaves, those who were worst placed worked for public institutions as road cleaners, sewer workers, road menders, builders, security patrolmen, or dockworkers. These slaves kept the cities clean and functioning but had few opportunities to earn gifts or money to buy their freedom.

A slave owner wanted to get his money's worth out of his human possessions. However kind he might have been he would still abandon any slave that could no longer work and often that meant that the slave starved to death. But treating a vast

number of slaves so harshly had a terrible down side. These multitudes of men and women had no hope but had every reason to hate. If they rose in rebellion they had nothing to lose but their miserable lives and the consequences for both slaves and masters could be disastrous. Writing about a slave revolt on Sicily in 135 BCE, the Greek historian Diodorus Siculus wrote:

Never had there been such an uprising of slaves. Men, women and children suffered and the whole island was near falling into the hands of the rebel slaves. It seems that the hatred of the slaves for their masters is increased as the richer, more luxurious and arrogant those masters become. And for this reason the masters are crueller, had their slaves branded, overworked, beaten and maltreated until they would stand it no longer. Their leader was a kind of magician and priest from Syria who boasted that the Syrian goddess appeared to him and told him he would be king.

Spartacus and the Slaves' Revolt

The most famous slave revolt is that of Spartacus, a Thracian soldier, who was probably captured on a battlefield. He was then sold to a master who provided gladiators (see panel) for the games. In his training for this sport he would have built on his military skills. Spartacus was a man of great courage and organizational ability as well as being a real leader of men. Between 73 and 71 BCE he led a revolt of gladiators from a training school at Capua. This rebellion was soon joined by other discontented serfs and his army numbered nearly 100,000 men. Spartacus had as little to lose as the household slaves who joined him in his rebellion, as he knew that as a gladiator he would eventually face certain death in the ring.

The penalty for a runaway slave was certain death and owners gathered together to hunt them down from time to time. Spartacus was too proud to die in such a manner. His vast army terrorized southern Italy and won several battles against Roman forces. It then began to march north, perhaps hoping to escape to Gaul—home for many of them. However, the conflict took the slave army south again. It took ten legions, which were commanded by Crassus, to defeat Spartacus at Luciana. Spartacus died in the battle. On the orders of Crassus 6,000 of the survivors were crucified along the Appian Way between Capua and Rome to set an example to any other slaves with a mind for rebellion. There were no more slave revolts on such a huge scale.

The Romans regarded slavery as a natural outcome of the fate the gods handed down to inferior people. Worse than the life of the farm slaves was that endured by the slaves sent to the mines or chained to their oars in Roman galleys.

SPARTACUS THE GLADIATOR

Spartacus was part of a legion of the damned whose life was spent in cells under the stadium or the circus. He would have been taught to work with a net and trident, a short sword and round shield, a spear and a dagger—all of which were used for close combat work. If he was to fight the wild lions from Africa, tigers from Asia, elephants, bulls and buffalo that were provided for the games, he might have only a long lance as a weapon and a thick leather belt as protection.

It was possible that if the crowd liked him they would allow him to live, even if his opponent had beaten him. They would demand "thumbs up" from the emperor or whoever was chairman of the games. These great and popular gladiators were well fed in comparison to other slaves and tended by doctors and masseurs. In the later days of the Roman Empire these men were the stars of the games and were showered with gifts and money that they had little opportunity to spend. The only way out of the arena was death.

As the spectacles grew larger and more exotic, men like Spartacus were adored by women—some of whom might bestow favors—and respected by men. But crowds were fickle and these fighters knew that one slip, one mistake and collective thumbs might turn down and they would be merely blood on the sand.

ABOVE *Roman gladiators confronting each other. One with a net and shield and the other armed only with a short sword. Terracotta, second century CE.*

RIGHT *An idealized picture of Spartacus fighting to the end when the slaves' revolt led by him was ruthlessly crushed in 71 BCE.*

Their only hope was a rapid death. However, Rome could not afford to let them all die. Slaves were an essential prop of the Roman economy and the mark of a man's worth. Any reasonably

RIGHT *Slaves were used as oarsmen for the Roman galleys where they sat chained to the oars and rowed to the merciless beat of a drum.*

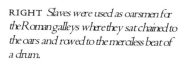

wealthy man in Rome would have slaves to work in his villa or his farm in the country. Well-born families needed at least 10 slaves in order to run the town villa alone. Men boasted of the numbers of slaves they owned. The historian Gaius Plinius Secundus (23–79 CE), better known as Pliny the Elder, wrote of one Gaius Isidorus, whose will claimed that he had left over 4,000 slaves to dispose of. Other well-placed Romans owned as many as 400.

Changing Fortunes

As the empire grew, attitudes towards slaves began to change. Some slaves proved they had more to offer than the work of their hands. While there is no doubt that many of the slaves lived brutalized lives there was a slow but growing movement to protect them from the cruel and arbitrary punishments meted out by sadistic owners. Old and sick slaves could no longer just be thrown onto the street nor could they be offered as victims to the men who organized the games. Much of the pressure for this came as a result of masters realizing that the men and women who were working in their households were sometimes highly educated prisoners from Greece or Egypt.

It was not unusual for such men to become tutors in the households of the wealthy. Better-educated slaves took on more complex and responsible work.

Doctors and teachers were often Greek by birth and training and any household that had one or both of these individuals was fortunate indeed. Some slaves even had the ear of the master, becoming the household's most trusted servant. Such an individual would be his master's eyes and ears inside the house. He might become a clerk or even be allowed to run the master's business matters. Cicero wrote on the death of a slave who had been his clerk that "[he was] more upset about it than anyone would suppose [he] should be about a slave's death."

The great philosopher and playwright Seneca (3 BCE–65 CE) had a personal slave who became a close and reliable friend. He reasoned that owners should treat slaves well as a slave was more likely to work hard and remain loyal to a kind master than one who continually beat, starved and branded his workers. Seneca believed also that masters and their families who expected their slaves to watch them eat well at a banquet and then only let them have scraps to live on, stored up trouble for the future.

> *The result is that slaves don't talk openly to the master; they talk about him behind his back. The cruel treatment doled out to so many slaves makes some people say that "you've got as many enemies as you have slaves." They are not our enemies when we get them; we make them so.*

Some of the female slaves had children by their owners and in some cases were lucky enough to be freed in order to marry their masters. If a slave could save the cost of his purchase, he could offer it to his owner and buy back his freedom. This route was normally open only to the slaves who worked in the households of the wealthy where

friends and relatives of the owners might offer such household servants gifts from time to time. As one of the few ways a slave might escape the situation such small earnings were guarded with great care. Freed men and women might continue working for their old master, either in positions of trust in the household or in an enterprise set up by him. A loyal slave might also be freed on his owner's death.

The Mighty Legions

CHAPTER X

WHAT DID SULLA, Marius, Pompey, Caesar and Tiberius have in common apart from being Romans? What did Octavian, Agrippa and Mark Antony have in common apart from being soldiers? Between 101 BCE and 117 CE they each led a Roman army to victory. From Gaul to Spain and from Egypt to Germany, from Greece to North Africa they commanded some of the best-prepared and most experienced troops the world has ever known.

From the moment the Romans determined that battle was the best means of defending their city they honed their army into a mobile and formidable fighting machine. From the expulsion of the Etruscans in 509 BCE to the withdrawal of Roman troops to Hadrian's Wall in 208 CE, the Roman army was almost unbeatable. In the early years of the city's history, Roman armies lost battles, but they always seemed to be willing and able to return to the battlefield unbowed. Slowly the Romans pushed back their enemies and occupied their land.

If armies are to succeed their fighting men must have a common objective, initially this was the defense of Rome. The young sons of well-to-do Romans faced 10 years of military service, by which time they should have learned how to lead men in battle. The commanders and their men were all Romans and self-interest spurred them on to defeat the tribes they confronted. Senators and other political figures were not exempt from command in the field and the men appointed as consuls expected it. ❦

OPPOSITE *A defensive battle line formed with shields by Romans whose enemy cannot break through. Note the auxiliary archers on the flank. A relief from Trajan's column.*

ABOVE *Roman legion in full armor advancing through a forest. Note that each of the faces seems to be a portrait. From Trajan's column.*

Each legion was a proud and independent element within the broader umbrella of the whole Roman army and competed against other legions for battle honors.

An individual legion treasured its standard very much as armies honor their regimental banners today. Every Roman soldier's sacred oath was to fight any enemy under command and not to abandon the standard. The penalty for abandoning this oath was death. Many died to protect the standard of their legion. Each legion was given a number and/or a name. If a legion was defeated its survivors were often sent into other legions and the number or name of the defeated legion was removed from official records as if it had never existed (see panel on the facing page).

Imbued with love for their legion and pride in their Roman birth the fighting men suffered rigorous training to bring them to perfection. The training was tough for veterans, but it was even tougher for new recruits. In battle new recruits were always placed in the front rank of the century and behind them were more experienced men. There were very practical reasons for this, as it allowed the new soldiers to feel that they could have confidence in experienced men who had been bloodied in previous conflicts and it prevented any of the new recruits from running away if they lost their nerve. If they did run there were only two directions in which they could go—onto the swords of the enemy in front or onto the swords of the men behind them. Perhaps the most cruelly pragmatic reason for putting the least experienced men in the front rank was that the most dangerous killing time was in the initial contact of the battle—if the battle-hardened and experienced men were at the rear they were less likely to be killed. As no army can afford to lose experienced men it was good military practice for the least experienced to confront the first wave of an attack. The loss of these men was not something to worry about and if a new recruit came through that first battle he knew what he had to face next time. He also had the pride of knowing he had survived his first battle with honor.

It was all part of the service Roman men gave their nation. Soldiers were not paid in the days when Rome's battles were relatively local, but this changed as the empire expanded.

Ambitious patricians knew that it was to their advantage to prove their courage and skill to the soldiers they led. And these men were well trained and battle-hardened. The army was their profession.

The Structure of the Roman Army

By the time of Sulla and Pompey the army was composed of small commands under the leadership of a centurion. He commanded a century of between 80 to 100 men. They were part of a group of 500 to 600 soldiers called a cohort. This in itself was part of a unit called a legion. Each legion had between 5,000 and 6,000 soldiers. The legion was the most important fighting unit of the Roman army and could act independently and with great speed and effectiveness whether attacking or under attack.

The Need for Change

By 146 BCE the Roman army had destroyed Carthage; in 102 BCE Marius defeated the Teutones at Aix-en Provence; in 86 BCE Sulla captured Athens; by 58 BCE Caesar was pushing

German tribes back and conquering Gaul; by 55 BCE Pompey had pushed into Spain and Caesar into Germany; and by 53 BCE Caesar had subjugated Gaul. The Roman Empire was extending its frontiers further and further.

As the Roman soldiers were taken further from their home city, the army began to use auxiliaries. These men were not Roman citizens, but knew that through loyal service they could achieve the advantages that citizenship brought. Soldiers from Crete proved to be fine archers, slingers came from other Greek islands, while Gaul and Germany provided fine cavalrymen. Julius Caesar particularly understood that it was not possible to keep up the numbers of men in military service just by recruiting Romans. He wanted to widen membership of the standing army. There were two ways he could do this—by extending Roman citizenship beyond Italy and into the provinces or by increasing the numbers of the auxiliaries by offering citizenship to those who completed 25 years' service and were honorably discharged. Indeed, as locally recruited auxiliaries proved their worth it was not unusual for most of a legion to consist of local recruits with only their commander a Roman citizen.

This meant shifting ever further away from the idea of a citizens' army, but despite this some of the Roman army's established traditions remained essential. Pride—in the unit, the legion's battle standard and in Rome itself—was an essential aspect of the military code that applied whatever a soldier's origins.

Officers

In the days of the kingdom and the early days of the Republic, military service formed part of a young patrician man's education. Throughout his youth he was expected to train in military skills and to know how to handle a sword, dagger, and shield. Because they were brought up in a tradition that honored their unit's past glories most young patrician men were proud to enter the army for a period of service. They would often lead men with as much as 20 years' experience—happy was the officer who listened to the advice of the veterans under his command. By the time his period with the colors was over a young patrician had learned skills of leadership that could be used to his advantage while governing his country as a member of the Senate. Men with ambition but

LOST LEGIONS

ABOVE *Portrait bust of the Emperor Tiberius. This marble bust was found in the amphitheater of Arsinoe in Egypt.*

In 9 CE Tiberius (42 BCE–37 CE), the heir of Emperor Augustus, led his legions on a successful campaign in Germany, after which he and his legions wintered along the banks of the Rhine. There was one tribe that the Romans still had to defeat—the Marcomanni who lived in the mountains of Bohemia. Tiberius was planning to attack them the following spring, using a pincer movement, which would trap the tribe between Roman troops on the Rhine and along the Danube. However, at a crucial moment Tiberius was called away to deal with a revolt that threatened Italy. He was succeeded by a nominee of the Senate, Publius Quinctilius Varus, who was a lawyer not a soldier.

The Germans realized his weakness instantly. Varus refused to listen to any advice and found himself surrounded by hordes of enemy troops. He lost control of his men, who were dispirited by his lack of leadership. Three legions were destroyed in a single blow and Varus committed suicide. The numbers of the devastated legions—the XVII, XVIII and XIX—were wiped from the record and never used again as the defeat was a matter of great shame. Roman prestige was dealt a terrible blow.

lacking in money could aspire to the highest reaches of political power if they had had completed successful commands in the field. Julius Caesar was one such example.

The Regular Soldier

The advantages of a spell in the army were clear for well-placed patrician men. For a regular Roman soldier there were also rewards. From the time of Augustus, Roman citizens signed on in the army for a period of between 15 and 20 years. They were paid and fed regularly and they had the promise of a one-off payment of 12,000 sesterces, a piece of land and a small pension at

RIGHT *Two soldiers moving into the attack covered by their shields. One with spear and the other with a broad-bladed sword. Provincial sculpture.*

RIGHT *Two soldiers moving into the attack covered by their shields. One with spear and the other with a broad-bladed sword. Provincial sculpture.*

the end of a lifetime of service, during which they could be sent to any part of the empire. However, it was a matter of fact that often the veterans had to threaten mutiny to get what they had been promised. There was an absolute ban on formal marriage for the regular soldier, although if he chose to marry on his discharge, his wife was given citizenship in her own right.

Tactics and Weaponry

The tactics of the Roman army were initially very simple and involved confronting the enemy head-on along a common front. Usually the Romans faced an enemy whose tactics were basic enough to allow this full frontal approach to succeed. A disciplined cohort steadily advancing across a battlefield must have been a terrifying sight.

As the men picked up speed they let go of a mass of flying steel shafts, which was often enough to cause the enemy to turn and run. The Romans would continue to advance and kill in waves. Men on horseback would then swoop in for the kill. If there was a need to turn the enemy flanks, more cavalry support was ready for action. The German tribes provided great auxiliary soldiers for such cavalry work.

Every soldier went into open battle with three weapons, each with a distinct function, depending on the phase of the battle. The pilum was a short spear, which was used to cause chaos during the initial phase of a battle. Legionaries charged at the enemy lines, hurling these killing spears as they ran. The pilum had a range of about 82 feet (25 meters), although some soldiers could throw it double that distance. In *The Iliad* Homer described the savage brutality of fighting with such spears:

> *...in the middle of the melee of men and arms and swords and flying spears Diomedes found his enemy ... He cast his hissing spear and took the Trojan archer Pandarus on the nose beside his eye. The spear passed through his teeth, cut off his tongue and came out under his chin. His burnished armor crashed as he fell from his chariot....*

These spears could hit the front lines of the opposing forces with astonishing power. They traveled swiftly and accurately, causing terrible slaughter in the ranks they hit. They had metal heads and wooden shafts. The shaft of a pilum broke on impact leaving its head stuck in a shield (or body) and rendering it too unwieldy to use. The Gauls were often forced to abandon their shields as a result of such an attack, leaving them unprotected.

Relying on the chaos caused by this tactic a Roman legion did not stop or regroup. The spear throwers next engaged in hand-to-hand combat. If repulsed they would retreat through the gaps deliberately left behind them and a second rank would take over the fighting.

The curved Roman shield protected both the front and the vulnerable sides of the advancing soldier. It was about half the height of a man. It was usually made of two wooden planks glued together with a metal boss at the center to deflect spears or arrows. In attack, the unit moved forward with the front and side ranks holding their shields

LEFT *Helmet, breastplates, leg guards and other trappings of Roman soldiers discovered near Naples.*

locked together and those in the middle raising their shields overhead to protect the men from arrows and spears raining down from above. This impregnable formation was called the tortoise. The soldiers used their short swords to terrible effect as they moved steadily forward into the enemy ranks.

To defend a retreating group of soldiers a third rank knelt behind their shields with spears pointing at a slant towards the enemy. They held

LEFT *The determined legionary was a ruthless killer in the chaos of battle where the Roman short stabbing sword made terrible slaughter.*

the butts of their spears in the ground, forming an impregnable wall known as the hedgehog. Behind this the units that had retreated through the temporarily open ranks regrouped.

Should the second rank also be beaten back then the third closed ranks and made a steady counterattack. Disciplined, steady and vicious they moved in using hand-to-hand combat while the other ranks regrouped and prepared to attack along the flanks. In this way the Romans kept a battle fluid and ever changing.

Like the Gurkhas today the Roman soldier's personal weapon was a razor-sharp, short, broad-bladed sword known as the *gladius*. This heavy steel blade caused terrible wounds. If the battle was so close that there was no room to swing or slash with a sword,

ABOVE *A bronze helmet found in Hertfordshire Mid-first century Roman British.*

a third weapon was introduced to battle. The *pugio* was a small stabbing weapon used to fight at very close quarters. It was deadly in the hands of the Roman legionaries. Killing, stepping forward, killing again and moving steadily over the dead, a Roman attack moved on like the well-oiled, well-drilled killing machine it was.

Machines of War

Inevitably the Roman army sometimes found itself with the problem of an enemy taking defensive positions behind stone walls, earthworks or sophisticated forts. To break through such

defenses the Romans copied the tactics that had been employed by Greek generals such as Alexander the Great who thought nothing of besieging a city for a year or more if necessary. The siege engines the Greek engineers created were so well designed that the Romans could do no better than copy them.

Siege towers were built of wood and covered by hides, which protected the attackers from weapons fired from the ramparts they were trying to breach. Once a tower was in place it acted as a bridge into the enemy position. Battering rams were also used. These were initially long tree trunks that were swung by teams of soldiers and were an easy target for the defenders of a city's walls. Arrows, boulders and boiling pitch could be rained down on the soldiers below. The Romans provided protection with a frame of hides that covered the soldiers. They also used a more permanent wheeled structure, which was rolled right to the gate of the building under attack. The ram was then slung from a beam, making it easier to batter down the door or the ramparts. At the same time this cover protected the miners who used pickaxes to destroy the foundations of the walls. Despite these tactics, it was inevitable that many soldiers died during attacks on such targets.

It was sometimes necessary to work at long range from a fortified position. The Romans adapted weapons that the Greeks had devised to beat towns into submission by hurling missiles at the walls and into the towns from a distance. The Roman weapons fired stones, bolts, barrels of flaming tar, a flammable mixture called "Greek fire" or other missiles into defended positions.

A complex and very powerful catapult called a *manuballista* was deadly when used by trained and skilled soldiers. It was essentially a hand-cranked catapult that was powerful enough to hurl an iron-tipped bolt with terrifying force and deadly accuracy into a breach in the walls, causing many defenders to be wounded or killed. It could also hurl huge boulders, tar or even diseased bodies into an enemy stronghold.

The *onager* worked like a slingshot. A lever was wound back using a windlass, then the tension was

suddenly released and the lever sprung upright firing metal bolts or flame carriers. This could rain devastation on a besieged city and cause chaos and terror among its population.

After such weapons had breached a defensive position, the legions followed with deadly effect.

The Legion

The key man in the training of the Roman soldier was the centurion. Like a sergeant major today he knew his men, realized their strengths and weaknesses and appreciated their likes and their dislikes. A centurion could be a soldier's best friend or his most vicious enemy. On his shoulders rested the prowess of the unit he commanded; if his century was disgraced in battle then he knew that a price would be paid.

The Roman army made pride and honor its greatest disciplinary weapon. Defeat or a foolish action by a cohort, legion or single soldier meant punishment. It might be loss of pay and privileges. It might be a loss of loot. At worst it might be a "decimation." For this, the most arbitrary of punishments, each man stood in line on the parade ground and called his number. Every tenth man took a step forward and was executed on the spot. A disgraced unit would be watched by other units. It was a cruel but effective means of ensuring that every man did his best.

When soldiers were on the move they lived off the land. They took whatever they needed and no one dared oppose them. If the people they left behind starved it was of no concern to them. If they lived in more permanent camps the nearby countryside would be denuded of cattle, grain or any food. Fodder for the horses was requisitioned from local people. No one dared complain.

Much of the time in camp was spent training, recovering from the latest skirmish, gambling, eating and drinking. Life was nasty, brutish and pretty short. The men kept fit because their lives depended on it. They moved across country like lightning. It is said that when Boudicca revolted in southeast England, a Roman force traveled from north Wales to London (approximately 700 miles) in less than a week to take her on.

On the frontiers from Syria to Germany, from north Britain to Egypt, Gaul and Spain there was the constant threat of an attack by the natives they were holding back. Even within the empire when states rose in revolution, it had to be put down. The legions did it—and they did it fast and ruthlessly.

If the soldiers were lucky enough to be garrisoned in a city or a town, matters were different. Permanent barracks were built for the soldiers and they even had some measure of comfort.

The Strength of the Roman Army

Professional generals were able to learn from battles of the past. Defeats and victories provided lessons for new soldiers and for experienced old hands and their patrician commanders.

When Julius Caesar chose to campaign in Gaul between 58–52 BCE he was not doing it only to serve the interests of Rome. He used the army as an instrument of his own ruthless ambition. Suetonius wrote that Caesar: "... chose Gaul as the place most likely to enrich him and to give him enough spoils and great victories to ensure that he would be voted a triumph on his return to Rome." Suetonius was writing with the benefit of hindsight in 110 CE, but he was right in his assessment of Caesar's motives. He intended to defeat Gaul and to push on to the next frontier if that would be to his personal advantage.

Once it knew its objective the Roman army would not back away. It was trained to achieve its target or to die in the attempt. It was a proud army and even the auxiliaries were as motivated as their Roman counterparts by the determination of their officers. If their leaders could bring them

victory and enough loot then the army would be their instrument in any adventure they chose. Caesar's determination in Gaul and the first battles in Britain made the army he commanded his personal fiefdom.

Rome's priorities were a safe frontier and safe trade with those it defeated. The priorities for the members of the army were loot, safety, survival and the possibility of a decent pension. That required a general who would deliver all he promised. Even the best of generals needs a measure of luck and a willingness to switch tactics in a moment. Alexander the Great could do it. Hannibal did it and Julius Caesar could do it too. Caesar brought a dogged, unrelenting patience to the battlefield that others may have lacked.

Above all, Roman commanders were able to trust their men to respond swiftly to new situations. They were willing and able to create victory out of disaster. It is the capacity to improvise, allied with attention to detail that made the Roman army the mighty power it became. Julius Caesar was probably the most skillful general to command the Romans. He was a master of improvisation and a commander with great foresight. Because he was victorious he was loved by his men.

Between the citizens' army that confronted Hannibal and the professional army that confronted Vercingetorix it is clear how much the military machine at the core of the empire had evolved. Between 219 BCE and 52 BCE that Roman army had become a formidable force. The vileness armies bring to those they defeat is perhaps best summed up by *The Iliad*:

Andromache wailed a wild ululation of pity, shame, anger and the horror of knowing her dead husband would not be properly washed and prepared and prayed over.

She unpinned her hair, letting it fall about her face as she knelt on the ground. She lifted the earth and poured it over her raven head. She raked her face with her long fingernails, to streak her cheeks in blood and took up more earth and poured it again to mix with the blood and cried out. "Your children have no father and I no protector..." And the sun fell dark beyond the mourning city...

The grief inflicted on Andromache at Troy was an emotion inflicted by Roman legions across their empire.

A ROMAN CAMP

The safety of his men should be the primary concern of a good general. The men respond by giving their commander their loyalty. Julius Caesar understood this above all and it served him well.

The military camp was designed to provide security and the main work was designed to ensure that an army at rest should be able to eat, sleep and dress their wounds. Even when the unit was moving out the morning after arrival the men built fortified earthworks, which can still be seen in some places today. On the march, toward the end of an afternoon a tribune with some experienced centurions would make a reconnaissance and find a suitable position to make camp. Ideally it would be on a hillside without any obstructions that could give cover to an enemy. Running water nearby was essential.

Having found a position and marked its center, a square was marked out and tracks running north to south and east to west were also marked. The ends of each track would be the gates in the wall that was to be built. Each unit already knew its place within the fortification. The officers were placed on the east to west axis. Alongside them the legions set up tents in two rows facing the track. Allies would be placed nearest the walls, which made them more vulnerable than the legionaries in case of surprise attack.

Once the camp was marked out the units arrived and the men immediately began to dig the walls, creating a ditch at the same time. The wall would have a walkway and probably a wooden palisade on the top. An open space was left from the walls to the tents to make sure the tents were out of range of enemy fire. Trenches were dug to serve as lavatories.

Such a simple, tented camp was the model for all Roman military forts. The more sophisticated camps, such as those along Hadrian's Wall, would have stone walls, watchtowers, exercise grounds, baths and formal meeting areas in the center of the camp where a general could review his men. There could even be a temple or at least an altar in an auspicious place. Store rooms for grain, oil and wine and areas for the sick and the wounded would be built too. Good roads were built to ensure the fast movement of troops across country or to reinforce allies or other legions at such permanent forts.

ABOVE *Soldiers busy constructing a fortified camp with high walls and wooden palisades. Note the walkways along the ramparts on which the soldiers can stand.*

The Legacy of Rome

CHAPTER XI

LOOKING ACROSS the land that slopes away from Hadrian's Wall in the northern reaches of the Roman Empire we are made aware of the distance the Romans pushed their boundaries. Beyond the line of stone walls, fortifications, small watch-towers and deep ditches lay the mysterious land of barbarians. From time to time sorties were made to keep these tribes in their place. Once a proud Roman legion marched behind their standard into the mysterious land beyond the wall. The legion was never seen again—they were totally swallowed by the barbarian maw. The Romans had come far enough. The troops manning this northern frontier of the mighty empire were, as often as not, a mixture of auxiliary forces from Gaul, Germany and Spain with only a sprinkling of true-born Romans among them as commanders. It was both a bleak and forbidding land they observed.

When Julius Caesar came to power in 49 BCE, the Roman Empire was continuing to consolidate its frontiers. It was a time when the city was unsettled and tension between the rulers and those they ruled within it was acute. This tension inevitably spread to the further provinces. Caesar understood that this had to be prevented or the cities and countries ruled by Rome would explode in revolution. The danger was close and it was essential for someone to take direct and draconian action. Caesar was the right man in the right place at the right moment for he dared to think the unthinkable. He imposed an undemocratic system of government by one man over the entire empire. ℘

OPPOSITE *The line of Hadrian's Wall sweeping across Northumberland at Cawfield Crags, which marks the northern edge of the Roman Empire (c. 117–138 CE).*

Having opened up the possibility of such rule, Caesar was followed by Augustus who was an even more subtle and ambitious man. Augustus disguised his autocracy by apparently acknowledging institutions that had held power during the Republic while in fact only paying them lip service. For some, according to the Roman historian Cornelius Tacitus (57–120 CE), Augustus left a legacy of chaos because his named successor, Tiberius, was a volatile, cruel and arrogant man. For others, again according to Tacitus, Augustus left a legacy of stability when he died. In the provinces Rome had provided a structure that the conquered people came to accept, because as long as they did so, peace, law and order followed.

The Eternal Empire

In Rome and beyond from Persia to Egypt and Spain to Petra, from what is now Iraq to southwest France magnificent buildings continued to be built, each more spectacular than the last. The great villas in England, France, Spain and North Africa were constructed around magnificent mosaics, fine porticos, hypocausts and tumbling fountains. Villas in the towns throughout the empire were similar to those built in Rome. The villas in more rural areas were clearly the result of great wealth and a feeling that peace was going to continue forever. They were not built as defensive installations or fortresses but were structures to luxuriate in. The men and women who inhabited these villas believed that Rome was immortal and they were building for the future.

The temples in Asia, northern France, Tripoli and Sardinia were an affirmation of this belief in the immortality of Rome's rule. Augustus began it by encouraging his stepsons to pacify the Germanic tribes and while they dealt with the borders of the empire, he consolidated his rule in the center. He began a campaign of building that glorified his rule, and in doing so he indicated to his subjects that the power of Rome was eternal. In some respects he was right, as Rome's influence is evident even in the present.

The Romans were a people interested in practical solutions to problems. Unlike the Greeks they were not innovative in literature, theater, painting or any of the plastic arts. The artistic artifacts that have survived were often the creations of foreign artisans and artists working in their home states while under the control of Rome. Mosaics in Roman houses were as likely to be designed and made by men from Greece as from Rome. The same is true of pottery, murals, and marble work, such as carving and sculpture.

The practical heritage that the Roman Empire passed down is most evident in the fields of engineering and architecture. From the vastness of the Colosseum to the elegance of the forums in Rome, Salamis or at Leptis Magna in Tripolitania, the empire's engineers and architects have left behind a record of practical and beautiful designs. Inevitably much of what has been left for us is martial in intent. Great triumphal arches such as the Arch of Titus or the Arch of Constantine span Rome's modern byways. As far away as Morocco the Arch of Caracalla still stands a few miles outside Meknes. There are columns that commemorate great men, among them the column of the Emperor Marcus Aurelius (121–180 CE); great marble bas-reliefs glorifying war and the feats of the emperors; baths and bathhouses from Pompeii to the aptly named Bath; and arenas in Arles and Nîmes, which still stand. All these are monuments to the glory of the rule of Rome and its military might.

Then there are the paintings that bedeck the walls of Pompeii and the House of Livia in Rome. There are the beautiful mosaics—a multitude of images in tiny pieces of cut stone that can still be seen in Paphos, Cyprus; in Eauze, France; in Cirencester, England; and in Turkey, Greece, Egypt, Iraq, Iran—all over the lands where this empire once ruled. These mosaics reveal images that display a rich profusion of harvest, home, temple, myth and legend. There are marble carvings that give us bullock carts, harvest and battle scenes, markets, bakers, water carriers, cobblers and butchers, cut into tombs, public buildings and temples to provide a wonderful and lively record of life as it was lived in the Roman Empire.

Rome effectively stopped its policy of expansion after the conquest of Britain by the Emperor Claudius (10 BCE–54 CE). Rome's victories as a result of the ensuing peace were even more remarkable. The civilization she typified spread over Gaul to the Danube, into Spain and North Africa, and the commonality of Spain, France, Portugal and Italy could be seen as the most permanent inheritance the empire left us. The Roman Empire was regarded with awe even

by the northern barbarians who eventually conquered it and took its systems of law and government.

Roman roads were a practical example of the way the Romans made use of local materials and created solutions to problems at one and the same time. It was essential that the Roman armies could move to any part of the empire swiftly. The system of roads built by armies of slaves and prisoners of war provided the straightest of routes for any legion to march on. No natural obstruction was allowed to prevent these roads from being as straight as possible. Roads like the Fosse Way in England ran straight and true for mile after mile. It is said that the news of the death of Augustus reached Spain within four days and that Caesar once traveled nearly 621 miles (1,000 kilometers) in a week over the Roman road system.

The Romans built for comfort and convenience and they were never ashamed to steal an idea from another part of their vast empire and to improve on it. Irrigation projects using the screw method of raising water were in use on the Nile for thousands of years before the Romans came. All they did was to introduce the idea to those parts of their empire where it was useful. The true genius of Rome lay in refining existing technologies. Their practical solutions still have applications for us today. When we consider saunas, flush lavatories, aqueducts, baths, irrigation, vast stadia, defensive walls, high-rise housing, water-driven flour mills, roads or public water fountains we are considering things that the Romans adapted and passed on.

What else remains with us from the Roman Empire? There are the poems and writings of many Roman poets and thinkers—who themselves owe a great deal to the Greeks before them. There are the sayings of Marcus Aurelius, who was both

ABOVE *The Altar of Peace in Rome on which carvings celebrate the city and the way of life during the relative stability of Rome under Augustus.*

GREAT BUILDINGS AND MONUMENTS OF ROME

The Altar of Peace is a magnificent monument to Rome and Augustine order. The frieze shows a procession led by the emperor and his family, followed by magistrates, priests and Senators, all of whom are going to make sacrifices to the gods. Each face is carved from life. This is not just a religious monument, but it is also a joyous affirmation of life and the benefits of Roman law and order.

The House of Livia may well have been Augustus's own house. One wall within it was painted in a style made famous by the painters of Pompeii. A stylized garden gave inhabitants of the house the feeling that the calm and peace of the countryside was not far away. The stability at the center suggests all the empire is calm too.

In Nîmes, France, is the Maison Carrée, a magnificent temple raised on stone to look down on the Forum. It is believed by many to have been constructed by Agrippa in about 20 BCE.

The Emperor Trajan (53–117 CE) was responsible for the Library of Celcius Polemaenus at Ephesus. In Djemila, North Africa, is the Temple of the Gens Septimia, which was dedicated in 229 CE. It was built by Emperor Alexander Severus (208–235 CE) and used as part of a new Forum. This growth of magnificent buildings went on all over the Roman Empire from the time of Augustus until the building of the Arch of Constantine in 315 CE. The list of baths, monuments, arches, theaters, temples, amphitheaters, columns, harbors and forums is a constant reminder of this once-great empire. Others include: the Pont du Gard, France, 19 CE; the Colosseum, 81 CE; the Theater of Marcellus; Trajan's Harbor at Ostia, 103 CE; Trajan's Forum, 111–114 CE; the Column of Marcus Aurelius, 172–175 CE; and the baths of Diocletian, 302 CE.

BELOW *The Celcius Library built at Ephesus, Turkey, by Julius Aquila in 135 CE, after restoration.*

emperor and great stoic philosopher; the poetry of Horace, Ovid and Virgil and the plays of Plautus. The Romans also developed a system of taxation; they created the three-course meal; they even gave us the calendar and the names of some of the months we use today.

Rome left us a vocabulary that was the common language of law, religion and learning until the end of the Middle Ages. Using this language, ideas were disseminated from one center of learning to another across the length and breadth of the empire even after Latin ceased to be spoken by the people. Monks, lawyers, clerks, traders and other men and women recorded daily life, mystical ideas, poetry, diaries, legal judgments, methods of trade and the daily grind of life in Latin. This language, in which so much of our history is recorded, is perhaps the greatest legacy of the Romans.

Decline and Fall

Edward Gibbon, the author of *The History of the Decline and Fall of the Roman Empire* (1776–1788) wrote: "It seems that all empires reach an apogee from which the decline is steady and often almost unnoticed by the people at the center of the fall." That was certainly the case for Rome. It was inevitable that the vast empire the Romans had once controlled would change and shift.

This arrogance and lack of doubt in Rome's right to regard itself as the only proper ruler of the world was in itself a canker at its heart that led to its collapse. In leaving behind a system where succession was by right of birth, Augustus left a legacy that was open to the political machinations of cunning men and women. Vicious gossip, the manipulation of the hierarchy at the core of the empire and unrest among the legions slowly sapped the strength from Rome and allowed the rot of the most powerful influences. It meant that the

rulers and the ruled were out of kilter with each other and that outside forces could also begin to change the power bases on which Rome had been built. Once power was eroded as a result of plots and machinations of politicians and military commanders or as a result of a weak emperor not controlling the activities of conniving families, interested political radicals or of the military, the days of the empire were numbered. But until then Rome itself grew and prospered.

Between the death of Augustus and the accession of Claudius a power struggle developed. Tiberius became emperor when Augustus died in 14 CE. Thirteen years later he withdrew from Rome to live in Capri and handed the running of Rome to an adviser, Lucius Aelius Sejanus. He was a malign influence and had already arranged the murder of several member of the emperor's family. While Tiberius was in Capri Sejanus waged a war of terror in the city until Tiberius ordered his execution in 31 CE. Tiberius himself died in 37 CE. He was probably murdered. His successor was Caligula (12–41 CE), who was a psychopath. Caligula ruled as emperor under the savage influence of his mother Agrippina. He was in power for a short time before his assassination, but in that time, "Little Boots," as the soldiers called him had demanded he be worshipped as a god. His sexual extravagances, wild parties and lethal abuse of power meant that he was little mourned on his death, but there was a problem yet again with the accession.

Claudius (10 BCE–54 CE) was the next emperor, a choice that was made by the Praetorian Guard who defended the city. He was badly crippled, had problems with public speaking and seemed to have preferred a quiet life. It was not thought that he could cope with the work or the responsibility. Yet when Claudius took power he acted decisively. He built a powerful civil service, ordered and completed the occupation of Britain and ensured that the processes of law and order were overhauled. Yet again, however, Rome and the empire were put at risk as a result of the personal ambitions of Claudius's fourth wife, Agrippina, who poisoned her husband so that her son, Nero, was guaranteed the succession.

The excesses of Nero (37–68 CE) are well documented, and the seeds of the end of the empire were now firmly rooted. Nero began his reign by pretending to look favorably on the Senate, but, as time went by and power ran to his head, he disregarded their advice and assumed the reins of power completely. He had Claudius's son Britannicus, a potential rival, assassinated and also ordered the murder of his own mother Agrippina in 59 CE.

After the fire that devastated Rome in 64 CE, and which Nero is said to have started, one of the first things he rebuilt was the wooden amphitheater where the games took place. These games were particularly important as a means of keeping the rabble satisfied with a diet of unutterable violence. Thousands of gladiators, Christians, criminals, slaves and political prisoners died the most terrible deaths in front of the many that flocked to enjoy the spectacle. This moral decline contributed to the downfall of the empire after the death of Nero.

Nero ordered the repression of a large number of patrician Senators and had them slaughtered mercilessly; yet he had no answer to the revolts in Gaul, in Spain and in Lusitania and as a result the Senate declared that the throne was no longer his. Nero killed himself in 68 CE and left the succession in doubt. After much bloodletting, Vespasian (9–79 CE), who had been a very successful commander all over the empire, was hailed as emperor. He came to Rome from Alexandria and began to establish order in the city. He was not a man of patrician birth and dispossessed the Senate of its privileges to promote his sons Titus and Domitian. As soon as peace was restored Vespasian ordered the building of a huge stone stadium, which would be known as the Colosseum.

The size of the building is an indication of the importance the emperors now placed on keeping the people sated and acquiescent. Three emperors, Vespasian, Titus (39–81 CE) and Domitian (51–96 CE), were involved in building the Colosseum. This magnificent building was 620 feet (188 meters) long by 500 feet (156 meters) wide. Its walls were 165 feet (50 meters) high. The corridors; arches; Corinthian, Doric and Ionic columns; shaded areas; galleries; and seats of the Colosseum were a vast architectural

achievement. The arena itself measured 265 feet (80 meters) by 178 feet (54 meters), with a wall and a deep gap between it and the seats to stop wild animals from getting into the crowd. In this arena men and women were sacrificed to the blood lust of the rabble in sword fights, net and spear fights, hunts, crucifixions, sea battles and women fighting dwarfs. Such bloody rape and slaughter was the apogee and the nadir of Roman Empire.

By 271 CE the provinces were steadily beginning to spiral out of control. It would take less than 250 years for the whole edifice to fall and for the fear of the early Romans to be realized. Their frontiers were breached on all sides by two new and more dangerous enemies than any that Rome had ever faced. One enemy, Christianity, already had a hold across the Roman Empire. But the second enemy preached the sword. The Goths were breaching the frontiers on all sides by 276 CE. And they would come with fire and steel. The enemy was at the gates of the empire and worse—much worse—it was also within. It was the end of the glory of Rome.

GLOSSARY

amphitheater Oval or circular building with rising tiers used for public games or contests.

annihilate To destroy; turn to nothing.

aqueduct Conduit for water.

auspicious Favorable.

auxiliaries Members of a foreign force that served Rome in war.

banishment Act of being expelled from one's home or homeland.

barbarians Outsiders considered inferior and uncivilized.

bawdy Obscene, lewd.

bellicose Waging war; belligerent.

betrothal Act of promising to marry.

capitulate To surrender or give in.

cavalry Soldiers mounted on horseback.

centurion Officer commanding a Roman century, part of a legion.

clique Exclusive group.

cohort Division of a Roman legion.

colors Armed forces.

concubine Mistress.

conspirators One who conspires; plotter.

consul Elected magistrate in the Roman republic.

consummate Perfect; complete in every detail.

denari Small silver coins in ancient Rome.

despot Ruler with absolute authority.

equestrians Group of tradesmen and merchants in Roman society.

eunuch Castrated man.

exploits (n) Notable or heroic deeds.

flanks The sides of a battle formation.

foment To promote or incite.

galley Ship propelled by oarsmen.

gilded Covered with a thin layer of gold.

Goths Germanic peoples who overran parts of the Roman Empire.

grievance Formal complaint.

grievous Characterized by pain, suffering, or sorrow.

harry To assault.

ides The fifteenth day of March, May, July, or October of the ancient Roman calendar. (Also, the thirteenth day of other months of the calendar.)

impetuous Impulsive; not given to temperance or thoughtfulness.

incursion Raid.

intrigue Plot or secret scheme.

legion Principal unit of a Roman army, consisting of about 5,000 to 6,000 foot soldiers plus cavalry.

lingua franca Common language used for commercial purposes.

magistrate Official who administered the laws in ancient Rome.

majordomo Butler; person in charge of domestic duties.

maw Gaping jaws.

oligarchy Government in which a small group exercises control.

ostentatious Pretentious or showy.

patricians Small group of wealthy Romans with political power and social standing.

perpetual Never-ending.

pilum Javelin or spear.

plebeians Common people within Roman society.

plunder To sack or loot.

portico Covered walkway or porch leading to the entrance of a building.

pragmatic Practical.

proxy Substitute or stand-in.

quaestor Low-level position of authority in the Roman republic.

ramparts Protective barrier.

reconciliation Restoration of peace or friendship.

sack To pillage.

treachery Deception; treason.

tribune Official in the Roman republic charged with defending the rights of the people.

tunic Simple, slip-on garment worn by Roman women.

turret Tower used to breach a defensive wall.

tyrant Absolute ruler who exercises power brutally.

vehemently Intensely; passionately.

verminous Filthy; infested by vermin.

vindictive Vengeful.

windlass Machine used for hoisting.

FOR MORE INFORMATION

American Academy in Rome
7 East 60 Street
New York, New York 10022-1001
(212) 751-7200
Web site: http://www.aarome.org
The American Academy in Rome is a center for independent
study and advanced research in the fine arts and the
humanities, set amid the classical tradition of ancient Rome.

Society for the Promotion of Roman Studies
Senate House, Malet Street
London WC1E 7HU
England
+ 44 (0) 20-7862 8727

Web site: http://www.romansociety.org
E-mail: office@romansociety.org
The Roman Society is a leading organization in the United
Kingdom for those interested in the study of Rome and the
Roman Empire.

Web Sites

Due to the changing nature of Internet links, Rosen Publishing
has developed an online list of Web sites related to the subject
of this book. This site is updated regularly. Please use this link
to access the list:

http://www.rosenlinks.com/pth/rome

FOR FURTHER READING

Baker, Rosalie F., and Charles F. Baker. *Ancient Romans: Expanding
the Classical Tradition*. New York, NY: Oxford University
Press, 1998.

Cowan, Ross. *Roman Battle Tactics 109 BC–AD 313*. Botley,
Oxford, UK: Osprey Publishing, 2007.

Everitt, Anthony. *Cicero: The Life and Times of Rome's Greatest
Politician*. New York, NY: Random House, 2003.

Goldsworthy, Adrian. *The Complete Roman Army*. London, UK:
Thames & Hudson, 2003.

Kelly, Christopher. *The Roman Empire: A Very Short Introduction*. New
York, NY: Oxford University Press, 2006.

Parenti, Michael. *The Assassination of Julius Caesar: A People's History
of Ancient Rome*. New York, NY: New Press, 2004.

Sullivan, George H. *Not Built in a Day: Exploring the Architecture of
Rome*. New York, NY: Carroll & Graf, 2006.

Ward-Perkins, Bryan. *The Fall of Rome: And the End of Civilization*.
New York, NY: Oxford University Press, 2006.

Zoch, Paul A. *Ancient Rome: An Introductory History*. Norman, OK:
Oklahoma University Press, 2000.

Index